Quilting

Patchwork • Appliqué

By the Editors of Sunset Books and Sunset Magazine

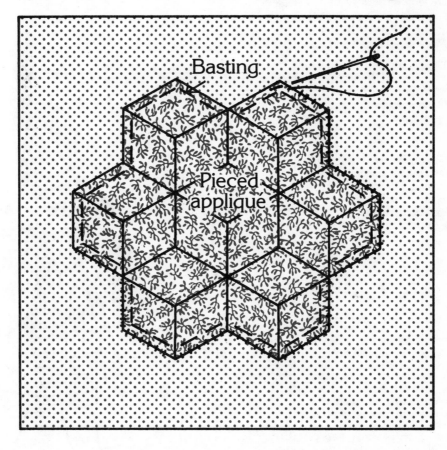

Lane Publishing Co. • Menlo Park, California

With appreciation to . . .

the quiltmakers, quilt collectors, quilt shop owners and others who were so generous in sharing quilts and quiltmaking ideas: Gail Abeloe, Marinda Brown, Lois Campbell, Karen Cummings, Suzanne Davenport, Marilyn Davis, Gloria Debs-Miyata, Edward Brown Gallery, Sandi Fox, The Granary, Margaret Hamlin, The Hammock Way, Glendora Hutson, Arla Le Count, Diana Leone, Mary Strickler's Quilt, Sylvia Moore, Charity Myers, Oakland Museum, Once Upon A Quilt, Patience Corners, Pierre Deux, The Quilting Bee, Esther H. Reilly, Santa Clara Valley Quilt Association, Santa Rosa Quilt Guild, Victoria Sears, Nancy Shelby, Heidi Weiss, Mary Whitehead, and Laurel Wilson.

And . . . a very special thank you to quiltmakers Roberta Horton and Lucille Hilty for their expertise and editorial contributions.

Cover: Detail of Baby Blocks Amish quilt, circa 1930, shows outline quilting and cable border quilting. Collection of Mr. and Mrs. Nicholas R. Cox. Cover design: Zan Fox. Photographed by Steve W. Marley.

Editor, Sunset Books: David E. Clark

Second printing June 1982

Research and Text:
Christine Barnes

Coordinating Editor:
Barbara J. Braasch

Photo Editor:
JoAnn Masaoka Lewis
Design:
Sandra Popovich
Illustrations:
Sally Shimizu
Photography:
Steve W. Marley

Contents

Patchwork & Quilting Techniques

Quilts are irresistible. The lure of traditional patterns and the sense of continuity they evoke, together with the excitement of contemporary designs and the potential for a new art form, all contribute to the current renaissance in quiltmaking.

If you take great pleasure in studying or collecting quilts, you're very likely to develop a longing to stitch your own. How to make a quilt, whether it's your first or one of many, is what this chapter is all about.

The women who gave us the tradition of quiltmaking learned at an early age; young girls began piecing quilts, often for their dolls, as soon as they could hold needle and thread. Later, quilting bees brought women together and helped perpetuate the craft.

Times have changed, and so has quiltmaking. Without earlier generations of teachers, most of us can learn quiltmaking only from written instructions and classes.

If you are afflicted with quilt fever, read this chapter for the basics of patchwork, appliqué, and quilting. Through your own quiltmaking, you'll soon discover the special attraction of this enduring craft.

A chronicle of quilting

Quilting could be Chinese in origin, or Egyptian; perhaps it began somewhere in the cities or countrysides of Persia or India. Certainly each of these cultures added its own refinement to the art. But wherever its roots, one thing is certain — quilting was born of necessity, of the need to keep out the bitter cold of winter and the chilly dampness of the rainy season.

Quilting in the New World

The custom of making quilts — stitching together two layers of fabric with padding between them — emigrated from the Old World to the New. Each Pilgrim family departed from the shores of Europe carrying complete sets of quilts — "bed furniture," as they were called — in preparation for the hardships ahead.

So poor were the settlers and so isolated from European conveniences that everything was used, reused, and reused again — including quilts. When worn, the quilts were repaired with scraps of old clothing and gradually acquired a completely new appearance.

Thus, though quiltmaking did not originate in America, one of its forms — patchwork — evolved from pioneer thrift and ingenuity. Those first worn, patched tops may not have been as beautiful as the tops we know today, but they were the forerunners of the striking and original piecework patterns of the 1700s and 1800s, designs that chronicled the history of the settling of North America.

As shipping lines carrying goods for the settlers were established, the seaboard housewife was able to obtain precious bolts of imported cloth instead of having to spin, dye, and weave flax or wool into usable lengths of fabric.

At this time, patchwork first established itself as a technique for the preparation of bed covers, prompting attempts at making pleasing color arrangements. In the warmer southern climate, covers were quilted purely for decoration and made from fabrics chosen not for durability but for beauty.

Restlessness and desire for open space carried many pioneers westward once more; again, quilts went with them. Exposure to new land and new experiences created new ideas in the minds of pioneer women. Patchwork tops became opportunities to express the happiness, the trials, and the uncertainty of frontier life.

After years of service, cherished garments found their way into the quilt top. Preserved in this manner, the personal history of a family could be traced from the oldest to the newest patch.

Quilts were very much a part of a woman's life. As a baby, she would be wrapped in one. As a young child, she'd learn quilting as part of her needlework training; a four-patch for a beloved doll might be her first endeavor.

In preparation for marriage, a young woman accumulated quilts in her hope chest. And this was no small task: customs varied, but 12 or 13 quilts were usually considered the appropriate number. The last and most beautiful, the bridal quilt, was not begun until the young woman was formally engaged; to start before that moment was to invite misfortune.

A woman's engagement was often announced at that era's great social event—the quilting bee. After marriage, a woman continued to make quilts to meet the needs of her growing family. The best quilts were often set aside to be used on the guest bed only and were then passed down to future generations as family heirlooms.

According to some experts, American quiltmaking reached a high point in the 19th century. Begun as a necessity, quiltmaking became a means of artistic expression. Women named the designs they created and traded their patterns. And their craft was aided by the growth of technology—fabrics produced in America were more colorful and cheaper than materials imported from Europe.

At about the same time, appliqué work grew in popularity. Once frowned upon as a flagrant waste of precious cloth, this practice of laying one fabric over another purely for decoration was now welcomed as a new way to embellish quilts reserved for special occasions. The careful storage and treatment of these quilts account for the number of appliquéd pieces displayed in museums today. On the other hand, not many of the patchwork bed covers that were in daily use remain for us to view.

Quilts as history

A study of antique quilts tells us much about their time period—what fabrics were available and how the quilters felt about them. For example, homespun was relegated to the back of a quilt when fabric could be bought. We can also trace the development of fabric printing from engraved plates and wood blocks to roller printing. Plant dyes gave way to chemicals, adding new hues to the quilting spectrum.

Studying a quilt can also tell us something about the quiltmaker. Many small pieces and tiny stitches

indicate a quilter with infinite patience. Indications of skill with color and composition vary widely from quilt to quilt. Some quiltmakers chose big, bold designs; others were more restrained—prim and proper. Some quilts were constructed by technicians, others created by artists.

Revival of quilting

The advent of machine-made goods marked the end of quiltmaking as a common household activity. Quilting and patchwork were revived in the 1930s and 40s, then largely ignored until the 1960s, when quiltmaking and other handcrafts were recognized for their freshness and originality.

Today, books, magazines, and entire stores specialize in quiltmaking, and classes are offered. People are designing their own quilts and once again meeting at quilting bees to share the work and exchange ideas.

This book offers information for the novice and inspiration for the more advanced quilter. If you're just beginning, don't tackle a king-size quilt as your first project; you'll learn more from completing several small projects within the same length of time. No matter what your level, sign and date your work so you'll be able to see and chronicle the progress you're making in your craft.

Designing a quilt

Quilt designing is easier than it first appears. To begin, you'll need to decide on the size, pattern, colors, and fabrics you want, as well as choose the general motif for your quilt. Even after you've made all these choices, you're not locked in. If the design doesn't evolve to your liking, you can—and should—make the necessary changes.

Project size

When making a bed quilt, determine exactly how much area you expect the quilt to cover. Do you want it to extend just to the edge of the mattress, or over the sides of the bed? How far toward the floor do you want it to reach? Will the quilt tuck under

the pillows or wrap around them? Also, remember that bed sizes vary —a water bed double bed, for example, has different dimensions than a standard double bed.

Consider also how much time you're willing to devote to the project. If it's to be a gift and your time is limited, you may want to sew large blocks. Another way to reduce the number of blocks you'll need is to center the area of the design on the quilt and add a series of easily sewn borders to the overhang.

Be sure to allow a little extra fabric for shrinkage from quilting. The amount a quilt draws up depends on the thickness of the batting as well as the amount of quilting.

The total size of the project may determine the size of the individual blocks or elements. A 12-inch block design in a double bed quilt may look better as a 15-inch block in a king-size quilt and a 6-inch block in a crib quilt. That's not to say that a 12-inch block *can't* be used in a crib quilt; consider each project individually, and rely on your own design instincts.

If your quilt is composed of blocks, you can determine the number of blocks you'll need by dividing the measurement of the desired finished quilt by the size of the blocks. To attain the correct finished quilt size, you may have to alter the size of your blocks slightly, or add dividers and borders (see pages 29–30).

Building a design

Though the quiltmaking technique you choose may impose limitations on your quilt's design, you'll still have to decide how to arrange your completed blocks. Some quilts are composed of individual blocks sewn together to form a larger, interrelated

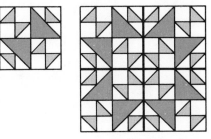

Old Maid's Puzzle

design. Others alternate plain quilting blocks with design blocks to set off the design and reduce the time required to make the quilt.

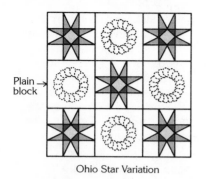

Ohio Star Variation

Stitching borders between blocks unifies the design and is particularly useful for a community quilt, where scale and color may vary from block to block.

You achieve a different design if you set your blocks "on point" rather than in straight rows. Setting a quilt on point makes the design appear more complicated; it also produces a larger quilt because the diagonal measurement of each block is greater than the straight measurement. With this method, you may be able to use fewer blocks.

Set on point

Design principles

Putting your completed blocks together in a pleasing arrangement will be easier if you take the time now to become familiar with some basic design principles.

Rhythm. A quilter usually strives for a design that keeps the eye moving smoothly across the quilt. An inappropriate spot of color can easily disrupt the rhythm of an overall design. For example, both yellow and red catch the attention and are better used throughout a quilt, rather than concentrated in one place.

Block placement also affects the flow of a quilt design. If a block has a definite direction, place it pointing inward—otherwise it will lead the eye off the quilt.

Balance. To create a balanced quilt, you'll find it easier to work with an odd, rather than even, number of blocks, particularly when design blocks are interspersed with plain quilting blocks. Using an odd number also provides a true center block, a necessary design element in some quilts.

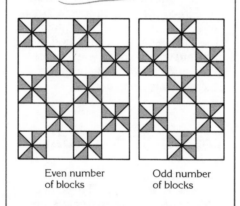

Even number   Odd number
of blocks   of blocks

If, once you've achieved balance, the quilt is not large enough, simply add a divider or border (see pages 29–30) to make up the deficiency—or set the quilt on point.

Unity. A finished quilt should look as if all the parts belong together. The more consistent the blocks, the more unified the quilt will be.

The sense of unity in many patchwork quilts comes from the repetition of identical blocks. When you study antique quilts, on the other hand, you'll find much less consistency, because the blocks were usually made with whatever scraps of

material were available. This inconsistency offers a folkart quality that is much sought after in a quilt.

To achieve unity in your quilt, you may want to use a limited number of colors or shapes—quilts needn't be complex to be beautiful. All fabrics can appear in each block, or only a few, if you're working with a large number of fabrics. If the blocks, when put together, are not as unified as you had hoped, add a divider in a strong color.

With the wide selection of fabric available, don't hesitate to experiment with unexpected colors or patterns. You may discover that occasionally reversing the coloring or adding an additional color or fabric will brighten and individualize your quilt.

Color as design

The most intimidating element in quilt design is also the most exciting —color. When you think of colors, consider both your personal preferences and the quilt's intended use. Though you may love a certain bold, bright color, living with it daily may be another matter. Quilters must also deal with the textile manufacturers' palette of colors.

The easiest way to think about color is in terms of a color wheel.

From the primary colors of red, yellow, and blue come all other colors or hues. Mixing adjacent colors on the wheel creates the secondary colors—orange, green, and purple. Adjacent primary and secondary colors can then be mixed to create the tertiary colors, for a total of 12 colors.

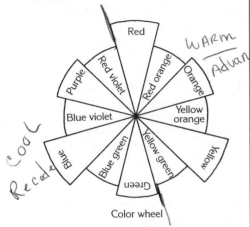

Color wheel

Neutrals—white, black, gray, and beige—do not appear on the color wheel. They may be added to a particular color scheme without altering the basic color relationship, since they don't count as additional colors.

Monochromatic (one color) schemes are the simplest; a patchwork quilt made from one blue fabric and one beige fabric is still a blue quilt. For more depth and complexity, you can include tints or shades of the same color. (Adding white to a color produces a tint; adding black results in a shade.) Your quilt is still monochromatic, but the various hues give it visual dimension.

Analogous, or related, colors are those that are neighbors on one side of the color wheel. An analogous color scheme adds vitality to a quilt while still soothing the eye.

Complementary colors are hues appearing directly opposite each other on the color wheel. The effect of complementary colors used in

equal amounts can often be dramatic. You can also use small touches of a complementary color to accent a predominant color.

Another way to look at the color wheel is to divide it into warm and cool colors. The warm tones center around orange; the cool colors center around blue. The dividing line would be drawn between green and yellow green on one side, and red and red violet on the other.

Warm colors advance and cool ones recede. Combining warm and cool colors in your quilt adds depth and interest.

Print fabrics

Designing with prints is more complicated than working with solid colors because the colors in a print combine to create a new color. One hint: look at fabric from a distance to view its overall effect. A small dot of color visible up close may not show up at all at a distance. You'll also find it much easier to work with fabric printed in just two or three colors rather than many different colors.

Scale is an important consideration in combining prints. If the scale or size of the prints is too similar, the quilt will appear monotonous.

Small   Medium   Large

To create an appealing overall pattern in your quilt, try varying the scale of the printed fabrics. Reserve the tiniest prints for the smallest areas, and save very large prints for big areas.

Density is the distance between the design elements in a particular print fabric. Varying the density of the prints you use will produce a stimulating design.

Design in a print needs to be carefully analyzed. Fabrics that feature a random, meandering design can be combined with prints having an allover design. Be cautious about using repeat motifs; rows of blocks made

from these designs can be distracting. Prints with geometric designs contrast nicely with the more typical calico prints.

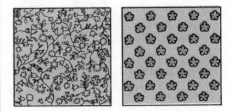

Allover design   Repeat design

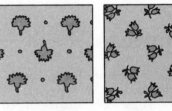

Straight rows   Diagonal rows

Specialty fabrics have their place in quilts, too. Fabrics printed in rows or stripes may be perfect for outlines or borders. Even a fabric that at first appears inappropriate for a quilt can be marvelous when cut up, especially if you're doing appliqué.

Once you're accustomed to looking at prints from all different aspects, you'll start buying fabrics that you'll use again and again. If, like most quilters, you collect fabrics, look for the lean areas in your collection and fill them in when you see the right fabric. Learn to rate your fabrics on their versatility in terms of scale, number of colors, and density. Fabrics with small-scale designs and a minimum of colors and contrast are the easiest to use.

A fabric that may not work in a quilt can make a fantastic quilt back. Though you'll want the backing to relate to the front of the quilt, some fabric combinations may produce a very distinctive effect.

Keeping prints separated from solids and organizing your fabrics according to the color wheel can save time and money. When you're ready to choose fabrics, it will be easy to pull just one section for inspection rather than rummaging through your entire collection. And if it's necessary to buy more fabric, you'll know what you're lacking.

The more you quilt, the more material you'll accumulate. Most quilters, in fact, tend to become "fabricoholics." To control this impulse, and to help you match colors when the urge to buy is overwhelming, you may want to keep a notebook of swatches of fabrics you have on hand.

Supplies

Old-time quilters needed only needles, pins, scissors, and thread to transform their fabric into useful bed coverings. Today, with the wide assortment of materials available, you'll probably buy most of your supplies at a fabric or quilting store, and some supplies at an art or office supply store. Below is a list of necessary materials, with helpful hints for their use.

Needles. Two important facts will help you choose needles: first, the larger the identifying number, the smaller or finer the needle; second, a smaller needle allows you to take small (short) stitches.

For quilting, choose a size 7, 8, or 9 quilting (betweens) needle. A quilting needle is short but permits greater control than a longer needle. Some sewers also appliqué and piece with this needle.

A size 7 or 8 embroidery (crewel) needle serves as an all-purpose needle for appliqué, piecing, and embroidering. This needle is longer than a quilting needle and has a large eye for easy threading.

Hint: Use a small piece of rubber (a balloon or a finger off a kitchen glove) to pull out a needle that's stuck.

Pins. Smooth, sharp, rust-free sewing pins are a must. Brass silk pins

are the standard, though some other types work as well. Several companies make extra fine, extra long, very sharp steel pins. Some brands have glass heads for visibility and easy handling; however, these shouldn't be used if you machine stitch over your pins because they don't lie flat in the fabric. Experiment—you may find that you use several different types of pins.

Hint: Do not leave your pins or needles parked in your quilt. The fabric and batting will corrode the metal and leave dark spots on your project.

Scissors. You may want to have as many as four pairs of scissors on hand.

For cutting fabric pieces, very sharp fabric shears are essential. They should cut easily and accurately through several layers of fabric.

Paper scissors are necessary for cutting patterns and designs; paper will dull good fabric shears.

Embroidery scissors are handy for thread cutting, which can form a dull spot on your fabric shears.

For small-scale cutting, such as clips in appliqué, use detail scissors with sharp points.

Hint: Never use pinking shears—they create a zigzag edge that makes it impossible to measure accurate seam allowances.

Thread. For appliqué and piecing, #50 cotton thread is recommended. For handstitching, work with lengths 18 inches or shorter.

Though polyester thread has replaced cotton thread in most fabric stores, polyester thread has many drawbacks in quiltmaking. If it's stronger than the fabric it's sewn into, polyester thread may eventually cut the fabric. For this reason, cotton-covered polyester is safer.

Polyester thread also builds up static electricity in your sewing machine, causing skipped stitches and tension problems. If you're sewing with polyester thread, clean your machine thoroughly with the machine brush or a clean toothbrush and remove all lint.

Use quilting thread for the actual quilting. It's very wiry and has a special coating to make it stronger. Polyester has now invaded the quilt-

ing thread market, but most experienced quilters still look for cotton.

Quilting thread comes in a narrower range of colors than regular sewing thread. Many quilters use either black or white quilting thread to make the fine stitching show up. Others try to match the thread to either the quilt top or the backing so the thread blends rather than stands out.

If you can't find a satisfactory color of quilting thread, coat lengths of #50 cotton thread with beeswax. Some brands of cotton-covered polyester buttonhole twist thread will work. Available in many colors, it's a thicker thread and will show more effectively in the finished project.

Hint: Thread spools are designed to be used on sewing machines. When handstitching, to sew with the natural twist of the thread and avoid knotting, thread your needle while the thread is still attached to the spool; then cut the thread and knot the end you've just cut.

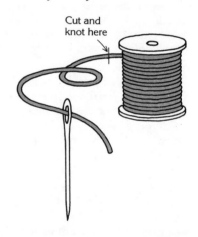

Cut and knot here

Thimble. Worn on the middle finger of your sewing hand, a thimble helps you push the needle through layers of fabric. Also wear it as a protection when you appliqué and piece by hand. Thimble-wearing is a habit— at first it feels awkward, but once you get used to it, you'll never be without one. Some quilters like to wear a second thimble on the hand underneath the quilt, too.

In addition to the standard metal thimble, you'll find ceramic, plastic, and leather ones. Experiment until you find the most comfortable one for you.

Hint: A metal thimble may conform better to your finger if it's bent slightly to an oval shape.

Wax. Beeswax can be used to strengthen your thread for hand-stitching and handquilting. Run the thread through the wax twice, then between two fingers to remove excess wax.

Hint: Keep wax in a separate container or compartment in your sewing box. Wax melts in hot weather.

Markers. For marking, use a sharp #2 pencil; softer pencils smudge and harder pencils may not mark on fabric. Washing, but not dry cleaning, will remove *most* pencil marks.

Many quilters use fine-point indelible marking pens for drawing cutting lines. These pens have the advantage of gliding smoothly over the fabric. But the ink may bleed when the fabric is steam pressed or washed, depending on the fiber content, weave, and finish of the fabric. Before using indelible marking pens, try them on a scrap of your fabric; then press and wash the scrap to see if the marks bleed.

Water-soluble pens save time in marking quilting designs. Read the package directions carefully and proceed cautiously. Some marks are permanent, though they are supposed to be water soluble; others reappear after they are presumed removed. Colored pencils can be used where a regular pencil doesn't show up. An artist's white charcoal pencil also works well.

Be sure to test all markers on each fabric you're using.

Rulers. You'll want to have several types and lengths of rulers on hand. You'll need both a 12 to 18-inch ruler and a yardstick for measuring and marking. A clear plastic ruler is especially helpful in designing and pattern drawing, since you can see through it to add seam allowances.

If you're cutting templates with a craft knife, be sure to use a metal ruler as a straightedge; plastic rulers nick easily. Metal rulers are also more accurate than plastic ones.

Square. Either a right-angled plastic triangle or an L-square can be used to mark squares and right angles.

Triangle   L-square

Iron. Pressing with a steam iron is very important in quilt construction. Make sure that the sole plate is clean so you won't soil the fabric. For best pressing results, test the iron's temperature on scraps of fabric. An iron that's too hot can melt and permanently warp synthetics.

For speedy piecing, keep the ironing board near your sewing area. Press with a terry cloth towel under your work for the best results.

Hint: Always store your steam iron in an upright position. Storing it flat allows any remaining water to drain out, corroding the bottom of the iron.

Frame or hoop. For many people, quilting with a frame produces a smoother quilt. No mysterious bubbles appear and an even tension is maintained. Full-size quilting frames are handy for large projects and quilting bees.

Small frames are also available; one of the handiest and least expensive is a 14-inch embroidery hoop. Try different sizes to find the frame that best suits your quilting needs. Your choice may vary from project to project.

Paper. Graph paper is especially helpful for designing and drafting piecing patterns; use large sheets with dark lines at 1-inch intervals.

Use tracing paper for copying a design. Cardboard and tag board, available at art supply stores, make good templates. Both wear down at the edges, though.

Acetate. A sturdy, clear plastic, acetate is available in sheets at art supply stores and some quilting stores. It maintains an accurate edge, and you can see through it, which aids placement on fabric. To keep an acetate template from sliding on fabric, attach pieces of masking tape on the wrong side.

Craft knife. Available at art supply stores, a craft knife is used to cut templates.

Compass. For drafting some quilting, appliqué, and patchwork designs, a compass is an extremely useful tool. Inexpensive compasses are not accurate because they will not keep a setting; choose a good quality bow compass that has two screws—one to keep the lead in place and one to keep the setting locked.

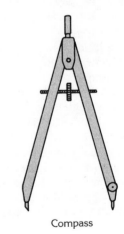

Compass

Community Quilts

Album, community, friendship, group, presentation—all these names refer to a quilt made as a communal effort. Few gifts can be more personal, yet practical.

In pioneer days, community quilting provided an excuse for women to get together with neighbors. Quilting bees, or what the Amish still call "frolics," were as important as barn raisings—in fact, these two social activities were often combined.

Gatherings started early in the morning and sometimes lasted until late at night, breaking only for meals. These days were hardly dreary—women congregated eagerly around quilt frames and stitched away while exchanging the latest news and recipes. Several quilts might be finished in a single day.

At times, friends exchanged individual blocks; from this trading of patterns came the friendship quilt—a quilt composed of separate blocks, each stitched by a different person, and the finished quilt presented as a gift.

A far cry from today's community quilt, with its planned-in-advance color scheme and design, those early quilts were wonderful collections of colors and patterns; often, a dizzying conglomeration resulted when all the blocks were stitched together.

Many of these quilts, each block signed by its maker, were intended to provide tangible memories. As families moved west, a friendship quilt became a treasured reminder of people back home.

Seldom put to use, most quilts were carefully stored away and retrieved only occasionally to recall different times—and old friends. For this reason, many album quilts are still found in museums.

Today, community quilting has expanded far beyond neighbors and friends getting together to stitch and set a quilt. Groups, schools, and organizations use community quilts to raise funds or to commemorate events. In 1976, many Bicentennial quilts were made communally to record 200 years of American history.

The quilts displayed on pages 80 and 81 are two fine examples of modern community quilting. Each of the Santa Clara Valley (California) Quilt Association members designed a block for the floral presentation quilt; motif, colors, and thread were chosen in advance to provide a unified appearance.

Sixteen scenes representing Oakland, California, were selected for the League of Women Voters landmark quilt. Dividers create a "shadow box" effect. Used for a fundraiser, the quilt is on permanent city display.

Another successful fund raising community quilt was stitched by a group of 30 women in Port Townsend, Washington. The Puget Sound town, with its stately Victorian homes, was "house rich" but "tree poor" when two residents decided to raise money to plant trees along city streets. A marvelous quilt depicting historic houses and buildings was designed, stitched, and assembled in less than six weeks; money raised from its raffle went to buy more than 1,000 trees.

But most communal quilts never earn a penny or a bit of publicity—they are projects such as baby quilts and wedding quilts made and given by groups of friends. Some are theme quilts—the organizer, for example, may distribute background blocks and instruct fellow stitchers to create an animal or a scene. Often the participants are simply asked to make a block of a certain size; the resulting quilt is as distinctive and special as the friends who make it.

Fabrics

A hundred years ago, quiltmakers had limited choices in fabrics. Cotton was most commonly used; wool, velvet, and silk were typically used for crazy quilts and some log cabin quilts. At that time, it was common practice to make a quilt with pieces straight out of the scrap bag. Many pioneer women were forced to practice a frugality unknown to us today—they simply had to make do with what they had.

Today we have many more fabrics available—natural-fiber fabrics, synthetics, blends, and knits. Many women still have scraps from their sewing projects, either out of tradition or just reluctance to part with beautiful fabrics. Many of these scraps find their way into quilt tops.

The problem with collecting scraps is that not all fabrics are appropriate for quilting. Fiber content, weave, weight, and scale of design are all important considerations in choosing quilting scraps.

Many quiltmakers can date their scraps to before and after the time they took up quiltmaking. Once quilting becomes an all-consuming passion, it begins to influence all your fabric purchases. You may, for instance, select a particular fabric for making a shirt because the scraps will be perfect for an upcoming quilt.

Whether you use scraps or buy all new fabrics for your projects, consider the following fabric characteristics as you plan.

Weave. Most cottons and blends have a plain weave, which makes them easier to work with than fabrics with a pile, like velvet and knit. Examine the tightness of the weave. Percale sheets are often used for quilt backs, but because they're so firmly woven they are difficult to quilt through. Some cotton flannel, though soft, is so loosely woven that it loses its shape quickly.

Avoid twill, a diagonal weave fabric. Though twill drapes well, quilters find that it stretches and is difficult to work with.

Weight. Your fabric's weight will influence the ease of quilting and number of stitches per inch. Very heavy fabrics are difficult or impossible to quilt; lightweight fabrics don't hold up well and may be too soft to use.

Fiber content. The most widely used quilting fabrics are either all cotton or blends of polyester and cotton. Cotton blends with 50 percent or less polyester will look and behave more like all cotton than blends with more polyester. To avoid differences in appearance and handling, use fabrics of the same fiber content in a project.

All-cotton fabrics wrinkle more than blends of polyester and cotton. Wrinkles are more visible in solid-color fabrics than in prints.

All-cotton fabrics have a matte finish; blends of polyester and cotton—especially those with more than 50 percent polyester—are shinier. If you're looking for clear, bright colors, you'll find many in blends, though all-cotton fabrics in bright solids and prints are increasingly available.

All-cotton fabrics machine stitch more smoothly than blends; the more polyester in the blend, the more temperamental the fabric. And for turning under seam allowances in appliqué, cottons will keep a crease better than blends will. All-cotton fabrics also ravel less.

With experience, you'll find that all-cotton is best for some projects, like appliqué using very small pieces and patchwork that includes curved pieces. Other projects may be successfully made in blends. Though cottons slip less than blends, it's often easier to mark designs on blends. Availability of colors and prints will also influence your fabric choices.

Prewashing all fabrics will help you avoid unpleasant surprises later on. Fabric that's washed shrinks—all-cotton shrinks more than blends do. Washing removes the sizing or starch in fabric; sizing gives fabric a nice appearance but makes it more difficult to handstitch.

There's usually excess dye in new fabric, particularly for the darker colors. Machine prewashing is better than washing by hand because the greater volume of water flushes the fabric more thoroughly.

Some dyes in imported fabrics will not withstand high dryer temperatures. Line dry imported fabrics.

Pretreating fabric. It's essential to prewash all fabrics in the same way you plan to wash the finished project. Naturally, separate lights from darks. If you fear that any dark fabrics will still run after one prewashing, wash them again (and again, if necessary) with a scrap of light fabric to check color fastness.

Fabric softener helps remove static electricity from blends of polyester and cotton, but use it only in the washing machine—polyester has a natural affinity for oil, and the fabric softener sheets that are added to the dryer may spot the fabric.

If you suspect that a fabric's color will fade or run badly, try setting it with vinegar. Using a cup of white vinegar to a gallon of water, boil the fabric for 10 minutes.

Quilt batting

A quilt is composed of three layers: a top, a backing, and a batting in between to increase the warmth. Cotton batting, once the most widely used, is now being replaced by polyester.

Because cotton batting is flat and unstable, it requires a lot of quilting to prevent shifting. If you like the flat, wrinkled appearance of antique quilts, choose cotton batting and take very small quilting stitches in closely spaced lines.

Polyester batting, more stable than cotton, requires less stitching. Quilting rows may be as far apart as 3 inches. A quilt with polyester batting is puffier than one with cotton, though the more stitching you do, the flatter the appearance will be. Because polyester insulates better, it's warmer to sleep under than cotton.

Polyester batting does have drawbacks. Sometimes tiny wisps of polyester come through the quilt top. Some quiltmakers have noticed gradual yellowing of all-cotton tops in quilts that have polyester batting.

Polyester batting comes in a variety of thicknesses; the thicker the batting, the harder it is to quilt. Very thick batting is most suitable for tied quilts.

Flannel and blankets can be used in place of batting. Flannel sheets can be quilted to give the flat appearance of cotton batting. A quilt made with a thick blanket will have to be tied; it can also be very heavy, but it's a good project in which to recycle an old blanket. Be sure to preshrink any flannel or blanket before you quilt.

Estimating yardage

Estimating the amount of fabric you'll need for the quilt size and design you want to make may sound like a chore, but careful calculations now will save you time and money later on. And you won't need to worry about whether or not you have enough fabric to finish the project in your original design.

To calculate yardage, you'll need to know how many pieces you'll cut from each fabric and how you'll arrange them for cutting. A sketch of your quilt design, a chart listing all the pieces, and a cutting layout for the larger pieces will help you with your calculations.

Quilt sketch and chart. Make a drawing—preferably in color—of the entire quilt design, showing blocks, dividers, and borders. Next to your drawing make a chart listing all the different pieces and the fabric used for each one.

Using the sketch, count the pieces and list the totals on the chart. Next to each piece, jot down its *cut size* (finished size plus seam allowances). Add several inches to the length of border strips.

Cutting layout. When you're cutting pieces of different sizes from the same fabric, it's helpful to "map" the cutting arrangement on paper.

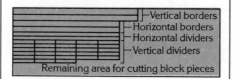

Draw a rectangle to represent a length of fabric, and label the width; to allow for shrinkage, subtract 2 inches from the original width of the fabric you plan to use.

Sketch a cutting layout for borders and dividers first, because you'll want these strips in continuous pieces. In the remaining spaces, fill in any block pieces to be cut from the same fabric. Note the length of fabric needed, in inches. To determine the number of yards, divide this figure by 36, showing the remainder in inches; round this remainder up to the nearest 1/8 yard. Note the yardage needed on your chart.

For uniform-size pieces that will be cut from other fabrics, it's not necessary to sketch each piece—a little arithmetic will give you the length of fabric needed.

Start by dividing the usable width of fabric by the cut length of one edge of a piece (for a rectangle, the shorter edge) to get the number of pieces that will fit in a row across the width. Divide the total number of pieces needed (see your chart) by the number of pieces per row to get the number of rows.

Then, simply multiply the number of rows by the cut length of the edge of a square (for a rectangle, the longer edge) to get the total number of inches of fabric needed. To this figure, add about 2 inches per yard for shrinkage. Convert to yards; note the yardage needed on your chart.

Sometimes triangles can be fitted together to form square pieces. When putting the triangles together,

remember to allow for seam allowances on *all* edges of the triangles.

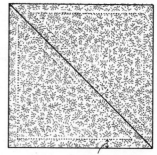

Seam allowance

For appliqué shapes, draw a square or rectangle that just touches the outside edges of the shape. Add seam allowances to all edges and treat this shape as a square or rectangle when planning a cutting layout.

Backing fabric. For a small quilt such as a crib quilt or wall hanging, one width of fabric may suffice for the backing. A larger quilt will require a seamed backing (be sure to trim all selvages before seaming). A sketch will help you determine the most efficient way to piece the backing.

If the quilt will be rolled in a frame, you'll need backing that's long enough to be tacked to the frame's poles; the backing should equal the size of the quilt top, plus 6 inches at the top and bottom edges, and 4 inches at each side edge. For hoop or lap quilting, add 4 inches to each edge. If you plan a self-finished edge (see pages 37–38), the backing should be even larger.

Patchwork

In the quilting world, *patchwork* is the term for sewing together fabric shapes to form a geometric whole called a *block* (usually a square). The blocks are then sewn together to form a continuous fabric, usually with a repeating pattern. Because patchwork involves piecing together shapes, it's also called *piecework*.

Pieced blocks are generally geometric and symmetrical; when well designed, they convey a feeling of balance. Most designs are composed of straight lines, which are easy to sew by hand or by machine.

Piecing is like assembling a child's jigsaw puzzle: a specified number of pieces make up the whole. But children's puzzles tend to be made with curved lines, whereas pieced blocks are usually composed of straight lines forming geometric shapes: squares, triangles, rectangles, diamonds, and the like. Designs such as a leaf, flower, building, boat, or tree can be produced by further breaking down blocks into smaller geometric units.

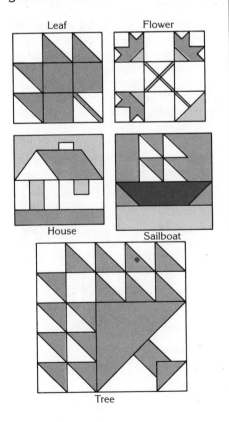

Leaf

Flower

House

Sailboat

Tree

Designs

When you first look at a pieced block, you may not perceive any order. Upon closer inspection, many blocks will reveal a number of smaller squares. If you can see these divisions (called the "grid" pattern), you will unlock the mystery of the patchwork design.

The simplest "four-patch" block is divided into four squares. A four-patch block may also be divided into multiples of four—sixteen squares, for example.

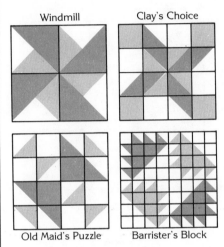

Windmill

Clay's Choice

Old Maid's Puzzle

Barrister's Block

Four-patch blocks

The most common "nine-patch" contains nine squares, three squares across and three squares down. In another version, each of the three squares is divided in half, creating six across and six down.

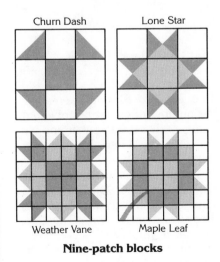

Churn Dash

Lone Star

Weather Vane

Maple Leaf

Nine-patch blocks

"Five-patches" and "seven-patches," unlike four and nine-patch blocks, refer to the number of squares across and down in the block. (A five-patch actually contains a total of 25 squares.)

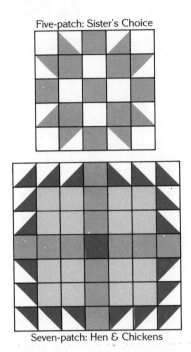

Five-patch: Sister's Choice

Seven-patch: Hen & Chickens

Patchwork patterns. Blocks that can be divided into the grid patterns mentioned above are easy to reproduce. Though paper folding was the traditional method for dividing a block into the appropriate grid, today's quiltmakers usually use graph paper.

If, for example, you wish to reproduce a nine-patch, outline a small version of the block on graph paper, making each square represent one square in the nine-patch design. Then draw the design on this small block. Also on graph paper, draw a square the size of the finished block (without seam allowances), and duplicate the design.

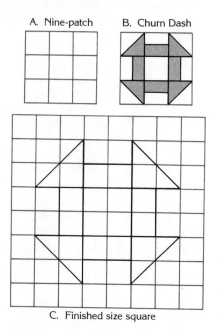

A. Nine-patch   B. Churn Dash

C. Finished size square

For simplicity, choose a finished block size that can be easily divided into nine equal units. For example, a nine-patch could be made as a 9-inch or 12-inch block: the 9-inch block would have 3-inch squares; the 12-inch block would have 4-inch squares.

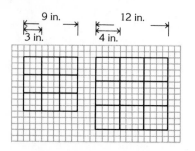

9 in.   12 in.
3 in.   4 in.

Once you've decided on a convenient block size, you can plan the dimensions of your finished work. This system works easily for designing a pillow; if a slightly larger size than the block is desired, borders can be

added. For a quilt with a repeating pattern, choose the number of blocks that comes closest to giving the desired finished dimensions. Dividers (interior bands separating blocks) or borders can make up a deficiency.

In a sampler quilt, where you mix block designs, make sure the *finished* blocks are all the same size. A nine-patch and a four-patch, for example, can both be made into 12-inch blocks.

Nine-patch   Four-patch

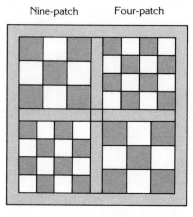

Sampler quilt

If you want to work with an existing design, determine the appropriate grid—the number of squares into which the block is divided. Repeat the steps above to draw the grid and fill in the correct divisions.

If you wish to create or experiment with a new design, start with a grid. For a simple design, choose a four or nine-patch grid; for more complex designs, use a five or seven-patch grid.

Light and dark. The use of light and dark values will greatly change the appearance of the block design. Fabrics of contrasting shades help define the design; fabrics of equal value tend to run together and blur the divisions within a block design.

Before you choose fabrics for your block, determine which shapes you want to stand out. Often the block can be divided into two planes—image and background. Traditionally, the image (or focal point) is darker and the background is lighter. Sometimes, reversing this order can enhance your design, so experiment before you make a final decision.

Pieced blocks of the same design interact in a quilt when placed next to each other. Together they form an all-over pattern that is not apparent when you work with only one block, as for a pillow. If you're designing a repeating pattern, try drawing the whole quilt to see how the blocks work together. You may need to change fabrics in individual blocks to achieve the desired overall effect.

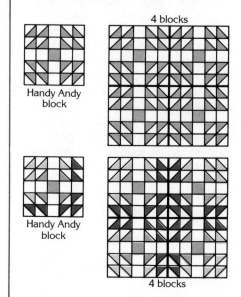

4 blocks

Handy Andy block

Handy Andy block

4 blocks

Color. The use of color can make a block look more complicated. Areas formed out of the same basic color will read as one unit; by using several colors within that area, you can sharply define individual shapes, giving the appearance of a more intricate design.

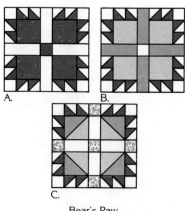

A.   B.

C.

Bear's Paw

Scale. Also experiment with scale. If a simple block is reduced in size, it appears more complex. Remember, though, that it will take more blocks—and more work—to fill the same amount of space.

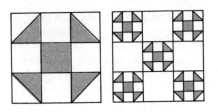

Churn Dash

Pattern preparations

Once you decide on a design, the next step is to produce a pattern for cutting and sewing. Having the design drawn full size on graph paper will help you.

Shapes and sizes. Analyze the design to determine the actual number of *different* pattern pieces. At this point, consider only the shapes (not colors) that make up the block design. You may need only one template (pattern piece) to guide the cutting of several different—and differently colored—pieces in your block.

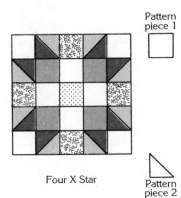

Four X Star

When you convert your design from a grid into pattern pieces, not all the grid lines will necessarily represent seams in the sewn patchwork. Areas made up of pieces of the same color can often be cut as one large piece.

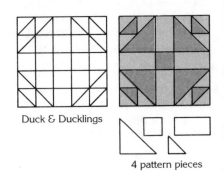

Duck & Ducklings

4 pattern pieces

Also consider how you will piece the blocks. If you plan to sew by hand, you may want to cut the pattern pieces so there are fewer seams. If you sew by machine, you'll find straight seams easier than corners; so you may want to alter the pieces in your block to create straight lines for machine piecing.

Farmer's Daughter

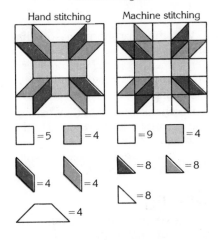

Hand stitching   Machine stitching

After you've isolated the shapes, *add a ¼-inch seam allowance to all edges* of the pattern pieces.

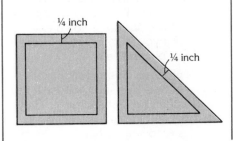

¼ inch

¼ inch

Cutting a template. Piecing requires greater accuracy than appliqué, so make and use your pattern templates carefully. Materials for templates are discussed on page 9.

To transfer your master pattern to cardboard, place carbon paper, face down, on the cardboard; lay the master pattern over the carbon paper and trace the design lines, making sure to include a seam allowance.

If you're using acetate, look for a kind you can draw on with a pen and cut with scissors. Place the acetate over your drafted pattern. Using a metal ruler, trace the design lines, making sure to include the seam allowance. Cut out the template with scissors.

If you can't draw on the acetate, tape your pattern on thick cardboard or on many layers of newspaper; tape the acetate over the pattern. Following the pattern lines that show through the acetate, cut the template, using a craft knife and metal ruler.

Clear templates tend to get lost when you're working on fabric. To keep track of them, place a piece of masking tape in the center of each template.

For precise handpiecing, you may want to make two templates—one for the cutting lines and one for the seamlines. First, make a sewing template the exact *finished* size of the piece. Next, make a larger template for cutting, with seam allowances added to all edges.

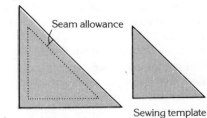

Seam allowance

Cutting template
(seam allowances added)

Sewing template
(finished size
of piece)

Use the larger template to mark the cutting line on the wrong side of the fabric. Then center the smaller template on each piece and mark around the edges for sewing lines. You can buy commercial metal "window templates" that combine both cutting and seamlines.

For machine piecing, a cutting template that includes the seam allowance is usually sufficient. Some sewing machines have a ¼-inch mark on the throat plate that allows you to sew accurate seams without marking seamlines. Merely line up the edge of your seam with the ¼-inch line, and sew.

Sometimes, the presser foot can be used as a guide, but don't assume that this is accurate until you measure the distance from the needle to the edge of the presser foot.

If your machine has neither of these two guides, place a piece of masking tape exactly ¼ inch from the needle.

Cutting pieces. Be sure to consider the fabric's grainline when marking and cutting pieces. Cutting the long edges of pieces along the grainline will help prevent stretching when you sew. This is easy with squares and rectangles but more difficult with other shapes such as triangles and diamonds.

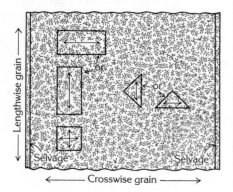

Think about how a shape will be sewn into your design. Try not to sew two bias edges together, though this might be unavoidable at times.

In some solid-color fabrics, particularly blends of polyester and cotton, the lengthwise grain can give a different coloration than the crosswise grain. Check the fabric you use, and be consistent in your layout. The color variation may not be obvious until the block—or worse yet, the entire quilt—is sewn together.

When cutting, try to be economical in use of both fabric and time. Cutting two squares right next to each other serves two purposes: less fabric is used than when a space is left in between, and less time is required to draw and cut out the two shapes if they have one common line. Multiply these savings by the number of pieces in a quilt—the result can be considerable.

With the very sharp scissors that are available today, several pieces can be cut at once. Marking is done on the top layer only; then layers are stacked, pinned together, and cut.

Do check your accuracy before you commit a lot of yardage to this technique; if the pieces are not correctly cut, more time will be required to sew them together.

Sewing

Before you start to sew, arrange your fabric cut-outs as they will appear in the final project. Better yet, pin the pieces to a plain sheet, or stick them onto a large felt board. Then step back and look at the design. Is the contrast good? Does the use of color interpret the design as you'd expected? If you're satisfied, you can go on to pin and sew.

Handpiecing. Some quiltmakers prefer to sew by hand because it makes their projects portable. They also feel that complicated designs are easier to sew by hand.

If you decide to handpiece your block, use an embroidery needle or a quilting needle. Sew with a small running stitch—8 to 10 stitches per inch—using thread that matches the darker of the two pieces being joined.

Machine piecing. It takes practice to piece accurately by machine, but the effort is worth it. Piecing by machine is faster and stronger than handpiecing, and the finished block is often indistinguishable from handwork.

Some zigzag sewing machines tend to chew up the beginning of a seam. To avoid this problem, use a throat plate for straight-stitching (with a circular hole rather than a slash) and a straight-stitching presser foot for greater visibility. If you don't have either of these, try turning the wheel by hand for the first few stitches. Then, with one hand, grasp the thread ends and gently pull them toward the back as you begin stitching.

Straight-stitching throat plate   Zigzag throat plate

Sew with a medium-size stitch—about 12 stitches per inch. Thread does not have to match perfectly, because it will show only in the seam. For sewing together many different colors, choose a thread that's somewhere between the darkest and lightest colors and use only this thread for all piecing; much time can be wasted rethreading.

Determine the most efficient way to sew the pieces together. For example, you can join small units to make a square, join the squares to form rows, and then combine rows to complete the block. In general, work up to the longest seams.

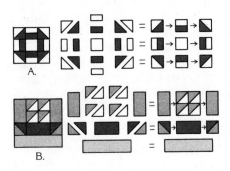

A.

B.

Pin pieces together, with right sides facing, before stitching. Place pins at the beginning and end of each seam and at points where seams meet. (Sometimes, small pieces can simply be placed together and sewn without pinning.)

Additional pins can be added, as necessary, to hold an area flat or to work in some fullness. When machine stitching, place the side with fullness on the bottom, and the feed dog will help ease in the extra fabric.

Some sewers stitch over pins; others prefer to remove pins as they come to them.

Press each seam after sewing, being careful not to stretch the fabric with your iron. Pressing seams to one side, rather than open, makes construction stronger.

When you sew small pieces into rows and then join the rows, seam allowances may meet in the row seams. To reduce bulk, press all the seam allowances in one row in one direction and those in the next row in the opposite direction; then join rows.

If you need to rip out a seam, cut every fifth stitch—the seam then pulls apart easily.

The placement of the quilting in the finished block may influence your decision on the direction to press a seam. In patchwork, quilting is often done ¼ inch from the seam, but you can also ¼ choose to quilt right

next to a seamline. Because it's difficult to stitch through the two additional layers of fabric in the seam allowance, it's best to press the seam allowance *away* from the area to be quilted.

Some pieced blocks also have an appliqué shape—a stem or a basket handle, for instance. It's easiest to appliqué before the block is completed; stitch the appliqué shape onto the separate piece, extending the raw edges into the seam allowance. Then assemble the block as described above. (For more about appliqué, see pages 22–29.)

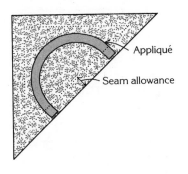

Appliqué

Seam allowance

Special sewing hints

Several shapes need extra attention—and time—to sew correctly. Below are hints for stitching pointed and curved fabric pieces.

Points formed by triangles, diamonds, and similar shapes with other than 90-degree corners present a special challenge. Usually, you'll be stitching more than two such pieces together to make a complete shape. Seam pieces only to the *finished* point and not into the seam allowance, to allow for the addition of other pieces. Make sure you mark the *finished* points; then begin and end seams at marks.

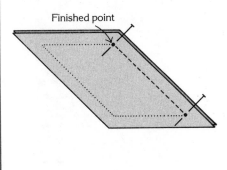

Finished point

Curved seams require special handling. Divide the curves, excluding seam allowances, on both pieces into fourths; pin pieces together, right sides facing, at these points. Add more pins where necessary to ease in the fullness. Clipping *almost* to the seamline on a concave edge may help in machine sewing. When you stitch, remember to place the convex piece on the bottom.

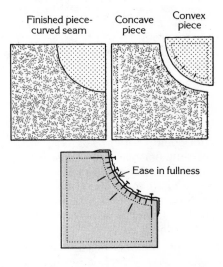

Finished piece-curved seam

Concave piece

Convex piece

Ease in fullness

Hexagons

Two popular patchwork variations, the hexagon and the log cabin, require some special instructions for proper construction.

Hexagons are an example of one-shape patchwork. Flower, honeycomb, and mosaic effects are possible.

To make a hexagon pattern, first draw a circle, using a compass. Keeping the compass at the same

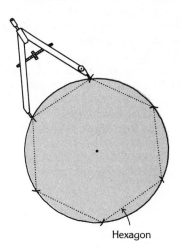

Hexagon

setting that you used for the circle, mark off six divisions on the circle. Join points with straight lines to form the hexagon.

Color is very important in hexagon patchwork. You'll want to experiment with pieces, or map out color placement on graph paper first.

You can sew hexagons in the same manner as other patchwork, or you can use the English method. In English patchwork, the raw edges of individual fabric pieces are turned under around a stiff paper piece and basted in place before the pieces are joined. This method results in precise edges, points, and corners.

To do hexagons using the English method, you'll need two templates: one the *finished* size of the pieces (for cutting paper hexagons) and one the finished size plus seam allowance (for cutting fabric hexagons). Mark and cut an equal number of paper pieces and fabric pieces, using the appropriate template for each.

Center a paper hexagon on the wrong side of a fabric hexagon; hold in place with two pins to prevent pivoting. Fold the raw edges over the paper, one edge at a time, basting as you go.

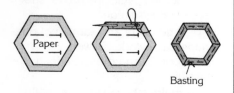

Basting

After you've basted several hexagons in the above manner, place the edges of two of them together (with hexagons wrong sides up). Using thread that matches the darker fabric, whipstitch one edge. Add other pieces until all have been joined. When you've finished sewing, press the entire work, remove the basting, and pull out the papers. They can be reused. The edges of finished hexagon patchwork will be jagged. To make them straight, you can appliqué the finished work to a square block, or you can add triangular patches to fill in the edges. If you want to preserve the jaggedness of the edge, back the patchwork with fabric of the same size and shape.

Log cabins

Log cabin blocks have a center square surrounded by a series of "logs" added in a certain order. The center square remains constant in size and color throughout the design. The logs become progressively longer as they are added from the center.

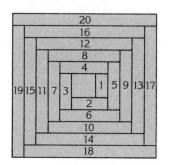

Though traditionally the width of the logs is the same, exciting variations are possible when you vary the width of these pieces.

The four basic log cabin block designs are spiraling, courthouse steps, chimneys and cornerstones, and off center. A popular related block is the traditional pineapple design. To choose a design, study the illustrations and descriptions that follow, and experiment on graph paper or with small strips of fabric.

The spiraling log cabin is the most common block design. To achieve the diagonal split in shading and pattern, use the same fabric for two logs that join at a corner, and a different fabric for the two opposite logs. The two fabrics may be light and dark shades of the same color, or of different colors, in solids or in varying prints.

After trying this simple construction, you'll see more complex design possibilities for the spiraling log cabin. For example, instead of using only two fabrics (one light and one dark) for all the logs, use a variety of prints and colors of dark fabrics for half of the block and a variety of light fabrics for the other half. Just be sure to use the same fabric for adjoining pairs of logs.

The courthouse steps variation is constructed by adding two logs of the same size and fabric to opposite sides of the center square, with log pairs increasing in length as they're added.

Alternate light and dark fabrics for an hourglass design.

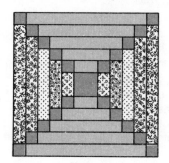

Courthouse steps

Chimneys and cornerstones design variations have squares where the logs meet at the corners. These squares can be at all four corners for an "X" design, or only at those corners that fall on a diagonal line.

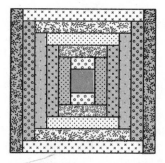

Chimneys

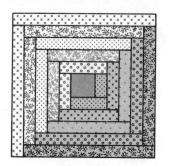

Spiraling log cabin

The finished design also depends on placement of color. You can divide the block diagonally with light and dark logs (as in a spiraling block), or place light and dark logs in opposite pairs (as in a courthouse steps block).

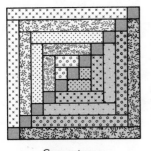

Cornerstones

Off-center log cabin blocks have logs of varying widths, resulting in center pieces that are not actually centered. Constructed in the same manner as the spiraling block, off-center blocks may have wide logs in one diagonal half and narrow logs in the other, or random-width logs throughout the block.

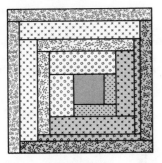

Off-center

The pineapple block, like log cabin blocks, is made by adding pieces to a center square. However, instead of straight logs surrounding the center piece, a pineapple block consists of trapezoid-shaped strips stitched to a center piece, with triangles added at the corners.

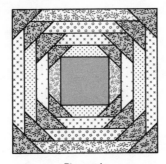

Pineapple

Finished log cabin blocks can be arranged, or set, in a variety of overall patterns. The two traditional settings illustrated here use spiraling blocks. You can experiment with other setting designs once your blocks have been sewn.

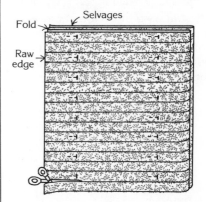

Barn Raising

Straight Furrows

Log cabin quilt construction can follow one of the three basic methods described here. For simplicity, these techniques assume you're using only two fabrics and are making a spiraling block. With an understanding of these procedures, it's easy to construct block variations.

To cut strips or logs, fold the fabric in half across the width; then fold each loose (unfolded) edge back to the first fold. Your fabric should now be in four layers, with accordion folds. Mark the desired width of logs (making sure to include seam allowances), pin, and cut *carefully* through all layers.

Fold — Selvages

Raw edge —

A tied log cabin quilt is built on a square of muslin cut larger than the completed block. Pin the center square in the middle of the muslin piece; lay the first log, right side down, on top of the center piece; pin. Fold the strip up so the fold is even with the bottom edge of the center and trim the excess. Stitch the strip to the center, open out, and press.

Rotate your work one quarter turn and repeat the process, using the same color fabric strip. This second strip should be long enough to cover the end of the previous log and the center piece.

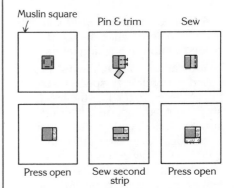

Muslin square | Pin & trim | Sew

Press open | Sew second strip | Press open

Continue the process, using two strips of the second color fabric, then two of the first, and so on, until all strips have been sewn onto the muslin. Press the completed block; trim off the excess muslin.

Sew the completed blocks together to form a quilt top. Cut batting and backing and combine the three layers. Using perle cotton or lightweight yarn, tie the quilt at the block intersections, following the directions on page 37. An "X" can be handquilted in the center square of each block to secure the layers and suggest handquilting.

A *quilt-as-you-go log cabin* involves the same process just described, except that you place a square of batting on a background block before you begin to sew.

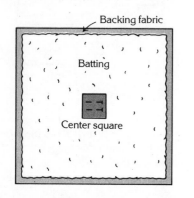

Place the background block right side down, then the batting, and then the center square. The background block will be the backing of the quilt, so choose a small, nondirectional print. Stitch with thread that blends with the backing fabric.

When the block is completed, trim the excess batting and backing fabric. Join the blocks, following the directions on page 29. A handquilted "X" can be placed in the centers.

A *quilted log cabin quilt* is made like a traditional quilt: the top is pieced without a backing fabric.

You can use a machine technique called railroading to speed up piecing of the quilt top. Lay the first log strip, right side up, on a flat work surface. Lay all your center squares, right sides down, along this strip, aligning the raw edges (as shown above right) and making sure to leave cutting space between squares. Pin and sew in one long seam.

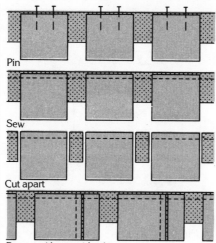

Cut the center pieces apart, using the edges of the pieces as your guide. Press seam allowances toward each strip. With right sides facing and raw edges aligned, lay these units along a strip of the same fabric to make a second seam. Pin, stitch, trim, and press as you did before. For the next two seams, use your second color fabric.

String quilts are related to log cabin quilts in that string piecing involves building a design, piece by piece, on a foundation fabric. Though the foundation is usually muslin, use newsprint for a fabric base if you want a lightweight finished string piece; once you finish stitching, simply tear away the paper. For the quilt-as-you-go approach, you can work directly on a piece of batting with a backing fabric underneath.

The strips, or strings, of fabric are cut in an assortment of fabrics and widths. You can sew strips so the

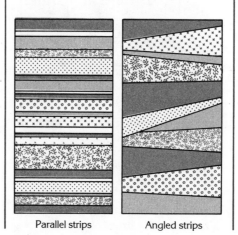

Parallel strips   Angled strips

edges are parallel, or angle the strips for a more interesting effect.

The foundation should be the shape you want the finished piece—square, rectangle, triangle, or diamond. A variety of designs result when you stitch completed sections of string patchwork into blocks.

To construct a section of string patchwork, lay the foundation fabric, wrong side up, on a work surface. Pin the first strip, right side up, on the foundation fabric. Strip ends should extend beyond the edges of the foundation. Baste outside edges of strip and foundation piece together.

Lay the next strip, right side down, along the inside raw edge of the first strip. Stitch these edges to the foundation, then fold the second strip right side up; finger-press the seam.

Continue this process until the foundation fabric is covered with strips. Turn the piece to the wrong side and trim the strips even with the foundation edges.

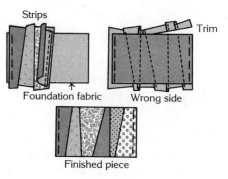

Finished piece

Quilt Care

Whether it brightens a bed or decorates a wall, your quilt represents many hours of planning and work. Realizing that eventually fabric deteriorates and becomes fragile and faded, you'll want to prolong the life of your quilt with thoughtful use and care.

Most heirloom quilts that are still in good condition were stored in chests and brought out only for special occasions. "Everyday" quilts of the past are gone or sadly worn and tattered. With common sense and caution, you can add years of life to your quilt and preserve it for a future generation's enjoyment.

Dirt, sunlight, and constant use all contribute to a quilt's deterioration. Below are some suggestions for washing, using, and storing your quilt to retard wear and tear.

If yours is an antique quilt, though, think twice before you wash it—old fabrics and thread are extremely fragile. If you aren't sure the quilt can withstand the treatment, do nothing. Better to leave it as it is than ruin it.

Dirt, whether surface dust or oils and stains from daily use, causes fibers to break down. An occasional gentle shaking removes surface dust; you can also tumble the quilt in an automatic dryer on the air fluff cycle (no heat) for a few minutes.

Dry cleaning shortens a quilt's life. If the fabrics were washed before the quilt was made, the best way to remove stains is by washing. The more stitching in a quilt, the better it will hold up when washed; extra threads support fabric when the quilt is waterlogged.

Whether your quilt is washed by hand or by machine, use warm (not hot) water; dissolve mild detergent in the water before adding the quilt. (Check quilt stores for special washing agents.)

If you're washing by hand, squeeze the quilt gently (never wring or twist), and rinse well. Rolling the quilt in towels absorbs excess water.

To wash by machine, use the gentle cycle for 1 or 2 minutes; turn off the machine and allow the quilt to soak for 10 minutes; restart and finish the wash and rinse cycles.

Never dry a quilt in the dryer. Let the quilt dry in the air, spreading the quilt flat, right side down, on a clean sheet, or supporting it carefully on parallel clotheslines. To restore the batting's loft, place it in the dryer on an air fluff cycle.

Sunlight fades a quilt's colors and weakens the fibers. If the quilt is on a bed, position the bed so it's not in direct sunlight, or draw the shades when the sun shines on the bed.

Rotating the quilt after 6 to 12 weeks of use and occasionally turning it over help preserve the colors and give the fibers a rest.

Continual use will eventually weaken a quilt's fibers. To minimize the damage, avoid tugging and pulling the quilt edges, sitting on a quilt, and folding a quilt the same way each time it's put away. Finally, keep your pet off the bed—the more stitching in a quilt, the more irresistible it is to a cat's claws.

Storage

When not in use, quilts should be stored in a dry, clean, dust-free spot. Avoid areas such as attics that have wide temperature fluctuations.

Ideally, quilts should be rolled, not folded, but a quilt may be loosely folded and inserted into a clean all-cotton pillow case or other clean all-cotton fabric, such as an old sheet. Never store a quilt in a plastic bag; fibers need to breathe. Also, quilts should never directly touch wood surfaces, whether the wood is bare or finished.

If your quilt is folded for storage, be sure to refold it occasionally along different fold lines. This is particularly important for heirloom quilts whose fibers are old and weak.

Appliqué

Appliqué brings to mind delicate, twining roses on antique quilts, and bright, bold motifs on more contemporary quilts and clothing.

As the word implies, *appliqué* consists of cutting a shape from one piece of fabric and *applying* it to another. In simple appliqué, you attach the shape to a larger background piece or block. More complex and versatile variations like multilayer, reverse, and pieced appliqué present endless possibilities for surface decoration in quiltmaking.

Designs

Appliqué allows the quiltmaker great freedom of choice — designs can be geometric and symmetrical or flowing and asymmetric. Whether geometric or freeform, appliqué designs are essentially silhouettes.

A metal cooky cutter functions in a similar way — it produces a shape in dough that is recognizable, but simplified. You know immediately what object the shape represents.

If you're doing your first appliqué project, consider large, simple shapes with a minimum of pieces; small pieces are more difficult to sew than large ones.

To create a simple appliqué shape, plan to use at least two fabrics. A turtle, for example, can have one fabric for the shell and another for the feet, tail, and head.

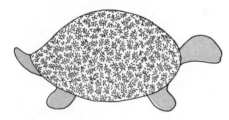

You can suggest a pattern on the shell by using a printed fabric; if you wish to make the turtle more complex, you can create texture and pattern on the shell with additional appliqué or reverse appliqué (see page 27). Choose solid fabrics for any areas that will be embroidered.

Embroidery

Enlarging designs. Many designs suitable for appliqué must first be enlarged. Most appliqué designs are centered on a background block and are slightly smaller than this block. (For beginners, a 12-inch finished block with a 10-inch appliqué is workable and pleasing.)

Background block too small

Background block too large

To enlarge a design, follow these simple steps:

1 Measure the widest part of design to be enlarged and draw a square this size on tracing paper. Cut out square and center over design. Outside edges of square should just touch widest part of design. Trace design onto square.

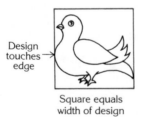

Design touches edge

Square equals width of design

2 Cut another paper square to desired size of finished design.

3 Fold each square in half; then fold this rectangle in half to form a square. Fold square in half two more times, ending with a square — you have now made four folds. Crease firmly after each fold.

4 Open squares. (Each will be divided into 16 squares.) Using ruler and pencil, mark lines along folds to form a grid on each square. Design you traced will now appear as if in a cage.

5 Place two grids side by side. One square at a time, check to see where design crosses small grid. On larger grid, place a dot at corresponding point on grid line. Work with pencil and eraser — enlarging moves more rapidly if you know you can erase.

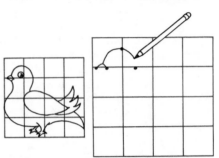

Continue with remaining squares; then join dots with lines. Or, if you prefer, work a square at a time, marking dots and joining with a line before proceeding to next square.

If design in any square is too complex to be transferred accurately, divide that individual square into fourths on both papers. These smaller grids will make it easier to copy detailed areas.

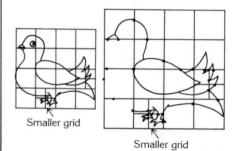

Smaller grid

Smaller grid

6 Look at completed design, going over it square by square to check for accuracy. This is the time to make any changes in the design.

Preparations

Once you have a full-size design, you are ready to reproduce it as a pattern for cutting the fabric. On the master copy you've just made, outline the design with a black felt-tip pen. This copy will never be cut up but will be kept for reference throughout the appliqué process.

Before making the individual pattern pieces, analyze the total design. Sometimes it's easier to cut and sew pieces that overlap each other rather than to follow the design as it's drawn. When pieces overlap, smaller pieces are first appliquéd on top of the larger part of the design; then the entire shape is stitched to the block.

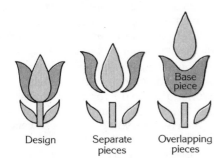

Design   Separate   Overlapping
          pieces   pieces

Decide how many separate pattern pieces you'll need. For pattern pieces that will be used many times, it's best to make cardboard or acetate templates (see page 15). But if you plan to use each pattern only a few times, use paper you can see through.

Lay the paper over your master copy and trace the outline, adding a ¼-inch seam allowance. If you want to appliqué by machine, or by hand using a buttonhole stitch (see page 24), do not add a seam allowance. Cut out the pattern. Pin the pattern to your fabric, and cut out the shape.

If you can see through your fabric, you won't need a pattern. Simply lay the fabric on top of your master copy and trace the shape with a pencil. Cut out the shape, adding a ¼-inch seam allowance.

Now pause a minute. Are you planning embroidery on any pieces? It's easier to embroider before the shape is attached to the background, and less puckering will result if your stitches go through only one layer of fabric. If you want to use an embroidery hoop, allow sufficient fabric around the design to fit the hoop.

One more word about embroidery: if you're going to turn under a seam allowance around a very small shape, or one with many fine details in the outline, consider first doing a chain stitch or backstitch along the *finished* (not cut) line that defines the shape. This line of embroidery forms a ridge that makes it easier to turn under the seam allowance and preserve the fine contours of the shape. The additional stitching takes time, but the result is worth it.

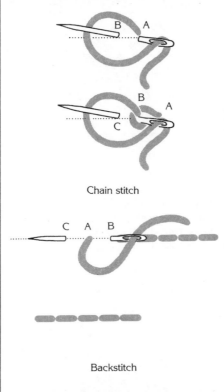

Chain stitch

Backstitch

You must do this embroidery before the shape is cut out. Use contrasting thread if you want the stitching to appear as an outline, and matching thread if you want it to blend. When the outline is com-

pleted, cut out the entire piece, including the ¼-inch seam allowance.

Cutting shapes. Many appliqué designs feature curved lines for stems, vines, and rings. There are two ways to cut these shapes. First, you can cut out a pattern for the curved line exactly as it appears in the design. This approach is easiest when there are only a few such shapes, but it usually requires more fabric than the second method, described below.

For more economical use of fabric, you can form long curved lines out of bias strips. For directions on how to mark and cut strips on the bias, see pages 38–39. Be sure to add seam allowances to the desired finished width of the curved pieces. The narrowest possible finished line is ¼ inch; for finer lines you'll have to use embroidery.

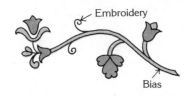

Embroidery

Bias

Cutting background blocks. You will also need to mark and cut background blocks. In appliqué, the stitching makes the block smaller. To allow for this shrinkage, cut your block with temporary ½-inch seam allowances on all edges. (Do not alter the size of the master design.) Once you've finished stitching the appliqué, you should remeasure the block and trim it, if necessary. Taking this precaution will save many heartaches, especially if more than one person is making the blocks, as in a friendship quilt.

You can also add a temporary ½-inch seam allowance to the outside edge of an appliqué piece to extend to the edge of the block. This edge will not be turned under, but will get caught in the seam when the blocks are joined to make the quilt top. (Baste raw edges of appliqué pieces and block together to prevent slipping when blocks are stitched together.)

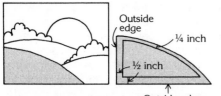

Appliqué stitching should begin ½ inch from the raw edge of the block — if stitching extends too far into the seam allowance, the knot may be cut off when you remeasure and trim the completed block.

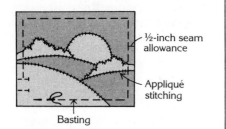

Once you've cut your background block, you're ready to transfer the design to it from the master copy. If the fabric is light enough in color and weight for you to see through it, simply slip the pattern under the fabric and trace with a soft lead pencil. For darker or heavier fabrics, tape the design to a window, tape the background block over it, and then trace the design — you may need to use a light pencil.

An outline of the design is usually sufficient; additional lines may show through the appliqué pieces once they're sewn to the background blocks.

A last look. You've cut out your appliqué shapes, your background block has been cut, and the design has been transferred to it. Before you go any further, arrange the appliqué pieces on one background block to see how the entire design looks. (Naturally, the shapes appear larger than they will on the finished piece, because the seam allowances are showing.)

Is there good contrast between colors? Can each piece be seen as a separate shape? Now is the time to

change a color or fabric that doesn't please you. If you're satisfied with the effect, proceed with the sewing steps below.

Sewing

For stitching, you can use either a size 7 or 8 embroidery (crewel) needle or a size 8 or 9 quilting (betweens) needle. Match the color of the sewing thread to the color of the appliqué shape unless you want the stitches to show as a decorative accent.

An invisible hemming stitch shows the least and provides the strongest application. Take stitches ⅛ inch apart, except on stress areas like corners and curves, where you should place stitches closer together.

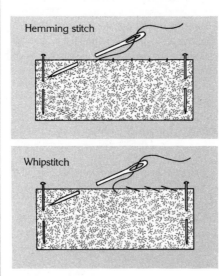

Hemming stitch

Whipstitch

To overcast a raw edge, try a buttonhole stitch. Normally done with several strands of embroidery floss, this stitch effectively outlines the appliqué shapes.

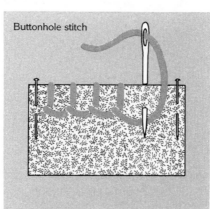

Buttonhole stitch

Determine which appliqué piece will be sewn to the background block first. Position the piece using the transferred design as a guide; pin or baste the shape in place.

If you attach with pins, always use two to keep the piece from pivoting. Remember, the pins are only to secure the shape for stitching; you're not turning under seam allowances yet.

Basting a straight line or an "X" will hold a large piece more securely. Basting around the entire outline of the shape is time-consuming and unnecessary. Often done too close to the edge, outline basting can get in the way when the seam allowance is turned under.

Once you've basted the first appliqué piece to the block, you're ready to turn under and pin the seam allowance and then begin sewing.

There are different opinions as to which edge of a piece to sew first. Working along the top edge allows you to smooth the appliqué piece more easily as you go. Some sewers prefer to start on the bottom edge — the one closest to them. Try both approaches; each requires different hand positions, and one will feel more comfortable for you.

It's best to pin and then sew only 2 to 3 inches of an edge at a time. (If the entire piece is pinned, it will be awkward to hold, and your thread will be more likely to get caught in the pins.) Turn under the ¼-inch seam allowance, and insert pins vertically 1 to 1½ inches apart, with the heads closest to the sewing edge. Remove the pins as you sew; then pin the next section, sew, remove pins, and so on.

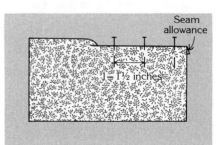

Check your work frequently: place it on a table to make sure your stitching is smooth. Also look at the back occasionally to see that you're keeping the background block flat. Mysterious bubbles can appear underneath your appliqué shape and can shrink the block.

Special sewing hints

Because appliqué designs vary so much, some require special methods. Below are hints for curves, corners, points, circles, and bias shapes.

Concave curves result when the edge goes *into* the shape. You'll need to clip such a curve so the seam allowance will flatten when it's turned under.

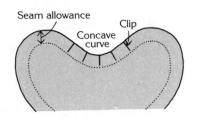

Clip less than ¼ inch into the fabric; make as few cuts as possible because they weaken the edge and may cause fraying.

It's safest to make a few clips, turn under the seam allowance, and see how flat the piece lies. If the edge looks too taut, pull the seam allowance back out, make a few more cuts, and try again. Clip curves only as you come to them—clipping in advance gives the edge more chance to fray.

On concave curves, use your needle to smooth under the edge just before sewing. For added strength, be sure to place the stitches closer together than you normally would.

Convex curves result when an edge curves *out* from the shape. Clipping convex curves is *never* done and, in fact, would make sewing more difficult.

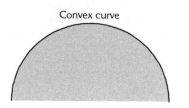

Turn under and pin the seam allowance at 1-inch intervals. Now work on the area between the pins. Because you're turning a longer edge into a smaller area, you'll probably feel lumpy folds in the seam allowance that form points along the folded edge.

To make the edge a smooth curve, place your piece on the table; with your nonsewing hand, position your index and third fingers on the folded edge and press down. Slip the needle under the allowance, pull up against it, and distribute the excess fabric that creates the fold. Pin the smoothed edge and sew.

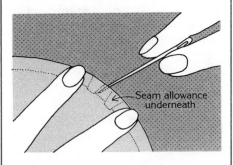
Seam allowance underneath

Corners require special attention. Turn under the ¼-inch seam allowance along one side of the piece; stitch to within ½ inch of the end. Turn under a triangle in the adjacent ¼-inch seam allowance; then stitch to the end of the first seam. Turn under the adjacent seam allowance and continue stitching, taking a few additional stitches around the corner to help smooth the edges.

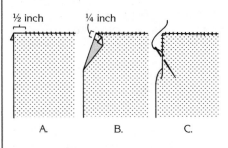

½ inch   ¼ inch

A.   B.   C.

Points are sewn in an almost identical fashion to corners. When the first seam allowance is turned under, it will extend beyond the edge of the

adjacent side. Trim this overhang to reduce bulk. Form a triangle, stitch to the point, and turn under the adjacent edge.

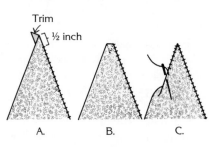
Trim   ½ inch

A.   B.   C.

If you're working on a very sharp point, pull on the thread as you're turning under the second seam allowance to keep the already sewn stitches secured.

Circles, particularly if they're small, can be very hard to appliqué. Here are some methods to try:

1 Before you cut a circle out, mark stitching line on it. Then cut out circle, and use marked line as a guide for turning under seam allowance and sewing.

2 Cut a cardboard template the size of *finished* circle. Place fabric circle, right side down, on an ironing board. Center template on fabric center and press seam allowance just over cardboard edge. With this circular crease, it's much easier to coax seam allowance under into a smooth curve.

3 Baste ⅛ inch from edge of seam allowance. Follow procedure in step 2 to make a circular crease on stitching line. Pull on basting thread to gather it around cardboard circle; remove cardboard. Basting takes extra time, but it evenly distributes fullness in seam allowance.

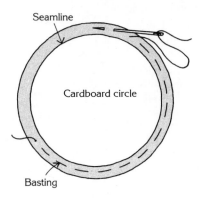
Seamline

Cardboard circle

Basting

4 Machine stitch slightly *less* than ¼ inch from edge around fabric circle. Machine stitching forms a ridge that makes seam allowance easier to turn under. Stitching will not show in finished circle.

Bias can be easy to work with if you remember one important point: bias stretches but will not shrink. (To cut bias strips, see pages 38–39.)

Always sew the concave (shorter) edge of the shape first; then, when the convex (longer) edge is sewn, the fabric will easily stretch to fit the area. If you sew the longer edge first, you will probably have to form pleats on the shorter edge to make the bias lie flat.

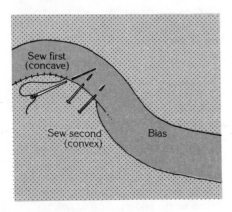

If you're working with ¼-inch bias (finished width), first iron under the ¼-inch seam allowance on one edge. Fold under the second seam allowance by hand, bringing it not quite to the edge of the first fold; baste. You'll then have an easy-to-handle ¼-inch bias strip with seam allowances already turned under.

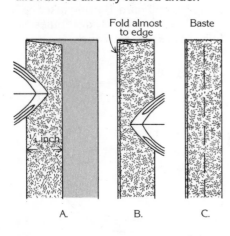

Appliqué variations

Variations on the appliqué basics produce dramatic effects in quilts. Once you've mastered simple appliqué, try the techniques explained below.

Multilayer appliqué consists of small shapes appliquéd on top of larger shapes in several layers. Because stitching through more than one layer greatly increases the chance of puckering, you should work with only one layer at a time.

Mark and cut the top (smallest) shape on the appropriate fabric. Mark the second (next largest) shape on the desired fabric. Sew the first shape to the second, and then cut out the second shape. Repeat this procedure until all the pieces have been appliquéd; then stitch this completed multilayer shape to the background block.

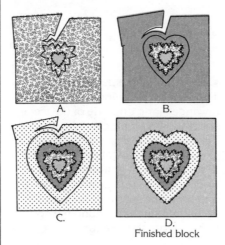
Finished block

Padded appliqué is useful if you want a shape to have a three-dimensional appearance. Lay your fabric shape on thin batting. (Batting and fabric will stick together.) Using the fabric as a pattern, cut the shape out of batting. Keeping them together, turn the pieces over and trim away the seam allowance only on the batting. Appliqué the two pieces as if they were one.

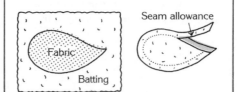

If you want to add decorative quilting within this area to stabilize the batting, do it before the block is sewn into the quilt top.

Three-dimensional appliqué can be accomplished with pleats and with shapes only partly attached to the background.

Form pleats in a piece before you appliqué the piece to the background block. When you cut out the shape, allow extra fabric for the desired fullness. Form pleats and pin or baste in place; then appliqué the piece to the background block.

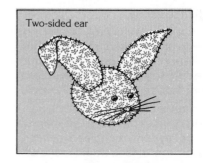

If you want part of the shape to be free from the background, the piece must be two-sided. Cut mirror images of the same shape out of fabric. With right sides facing, stitch the edges together, leaving an opening; turn the piece to the right side. Then turn in the seam allowance, sew it closed, and partially appliqué this piece to the design.

Two-sided ear

Because three-dimensional appliqué shows wear more quickly than flat appliqué, you'll want to consider the intended use of the quilt before you decorate it with either method.

Reverse appliqué is the technique used by the Cuna Indians of the San Blas Islands off Panama to produce the popular, colorful *molas*.

In reverse appliqué, the top layer is cut through to expose fabrics underneath. A separate layer is needed for each color in the design. Reverse appliqué is particularly appropriate where a small shape of color, such as a slash or circle, is called for.

Fabric selection is very important in this technique. Choose a smooth, finely woven fabric that doesn't fray. All-cotton fabric works best because it holds a firm crease.

To do reverse appliqué in the traditional manner, first mark the design on the top fabric. For an interior cut-out area, such as a flower center, cut out the shape carefully, remembering to allow extra fabric for a seam allowance to turn under (A). (The cut-out area will be *smaller* than the finished shape.)

Cut a square of fabric in the color you want to show through the opening (B). Don't be skimpy; allow enough fabric to make positioning and sewing of this piece easy. Pin and baste the piece underneath the opening; make sure basting is at least ½ inch away from cut edge. Turn under the seam allowance at the cut-out edges on the large piece (clipping where necessary), and sew. Use your needle to tuck under any frayed threads and make the edge smooth. Press lightly from the top; turn to the back, remove basting, and trim away excess fabric from the smaller piece.

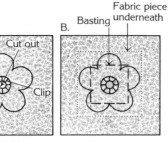

Cut out the entire design, being careful to include a seam allowance to turn under (C). Appliqué this piece to the background fabric (D).

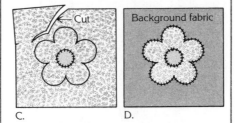

You can also do reverse appliqué by cutting all layers of fabric the same size as the top layer. An incision is made with sharp scissors through the top fabric and each layer until the appropriate color shows. The bottom layer is never cut; it acts as a lining. The finished result is bulky and allows only a minimum of quilting.

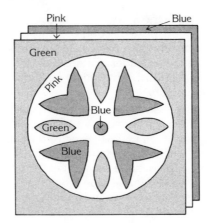

Pieced appliqué involves a shape that is made up of smaller pieces and that doesn't by itself form a square when finished. This pieced shape is basted and appliquéd to a background block. To make quilting

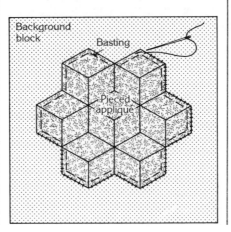

on a pieced shape easier, turn the block to the back and carefully cut away the background fabric that lies *underneath* the shape. Do not trim the background fabric too close to the appliqué stitching, or the stitching may not hold.

Crazy quilts, the Victorian rage, are not really quilts in the traditional sense. A combination of appliqué and embroidery, they rarely have batting or quilting, though some are tied inconspicuously from the back. Crazy quilt tops are composed of foundation blocks covered with pieces in random shapes, fabrics, and colors. On most crazy quilts, embroidery embellishes the seams.

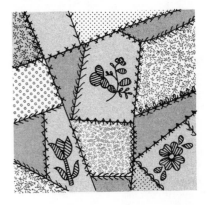

Victorian crazy quilts were made from scraps of opulent fabric—satins, silks, and velvet. You can choose a variety of fabric weights and textures, but keep in mind that solid color or small-scale fabrics will best display the finishing embroidery.

Unlike other quilts, a crazy quilt can be designed as you go. Or if you prefer to plan ahead, make a pattern by drawing the shapes you want on a square of paper; then cut it into pattern pieces. Be sure to add seam allowances to the pattern pieces.

The irregular-shaped pieces are stitched to a foundation block cut from muslin.

Starting in the upper left-hand corner, pin the first fabric shape in place, right side up. Baste the outer edges of this piece to the block. Pieces may be added in any of the following ways:

• To appliqué in the traditional fashion, pin the second piece in place, turning under a seam allowance and overlapping the raw edge of the first piece. Baste close to the fold through all thicknesses (you'll remove the basting after you've done the embroidery); or sew the first piece to the second with an invisible hemming stitch (see page 24).

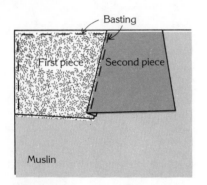

The pieces can be different sizes and shapes—even curved; just be sure that the edge of each piece overlaps the previous one enough to prevent raveling. Continue overlapping and stitching pieces until the entire foundation block is covered.

• To appliqué by machine, overlap the raw edges of the pieces slightly and sew with a zigzag stitch.

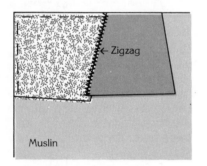

• Another appliqué technique is very similar to that used for string quilts (see page 20). Place the second piece, right side down, along the raw edge of the first piece. Using a ¼-inch seam allowance and stitching by hand or machine, sew the edges through all thicknesses.

Fold the second piece right side up, and finger-press the seam. Continue adding pieces until the foundation piece is covered. With this technique, all seams must be straight, though you can vary the angle and width of the pieces.

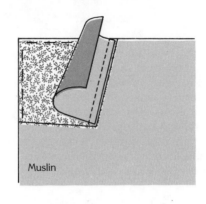

Once the foundation piece is covered, baste around the outside edges and trim pieces even with the foundation edges. Embroider the seamlines using a variety of stitches and colors.

Because of the embroidery, quilting is not practical on a crazy quilt project. You can either leave the top and backing free (attached only at the edges), or tie the quilt at the corners of the foundation blocks (see page 37), working from the back so the knots don't show.

Machine appliqué is much faster than appliqué done by hand, but there are noticeable differences in the finished appearance of machine zigzag stitching and handwork. Machine appliqué stands out more than handstitching and becomes an important decorative element in a quilt.

Another difference is that machine stitching flattens the appliqué shape. Experiment with machine appliqué to see its effects before you commit yourself to this technique for an entire project.

The width of the stitching depends on the weight of the background fabric—the more lightweight the fabric, the narrower the stitch should be. If this technique is new to you, you'll get the best results using medium-weight fabric and a relatively wide stitch.

Stitch length is equally important—stitches should be as close as possible without bunching. Whatever width and length you choose, stitching should be smooth and rounded, with no bobbin thread showing.

With machine appliqué, you don't turn under the edges, so you'll cut each appliqué shape the *finished* size, without a seam allowance (see exception below).

There are several ways to appliqué by machine; experiment with each one, choose the method you like best, and then *practice* before starting your project. *One stitching hint that applies to all three approaches: when turning corners, leave the needle in the background fabric, raise the presser foot, and pivot your work.*

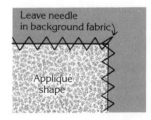

• The most straightforward method is to baste each cut shape in place by hand, then zigzag over the raw edges.

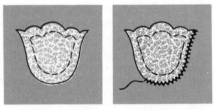

Baste by hand   Zigzag

• You can also appliqué a shape and trim it. Draw the shape on fabric; cut it out, leaving a ½-inch allowance at the edges. Pin the shape on the background and machine stitch, using a regular stitch, along the marked line. Trim as close as possible to the stitching line; zigzag over the stitching.

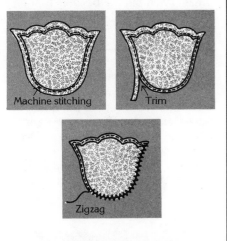
Machine stitching
Trim
Zigzag

- Bonding a shape to the background before stitching ensures a smooth appliqué, especially if the shape is large. Cut fusible web slightly smaller than the appliqué shape; fuse the shape to the background according to the package instructions. (Be careful not to get any web on your iron.) Zigzag over the raw edges.

Plastic bags used to cover dry-cleaned garments also work as bonding, though you should pretest with your fabrics. Cut the plastic slightly larger than the appliqué shape; sandwich the plastic between the shape and the background. Completely cover your work with paper towels; then iron. (Paper towels will absorb the excess plastic.) Zigzag over the raw edges.

Setting a quilt top

"Setting" a quilt refers to the way you join the design elements to form the quilt top. The easiest method is to sew block to block, but you can also alternate design blocks with plain blocks, separate blocks with dividers, or set the blocks on point. For a more detailed discussion of design considerations, see "Building a design," pages 5–6.

Joining blocks

Take your choice of two basic methods for assembling a quilt— traditional or quilt-as-you-go.

The traditional approach is to construct the entire quilt top, then quilt it to the backing and batting. In the quilt-as-you-go method, you quilt one block at a time.

From the front of the quilt, you should not be able to tell which method of construction was used. However, quilt-as-you-go quilts will have many more seams on the back, and the finished quilt will not be as strong as one with a solid backing. Also, though the quilt-as-you-go method allows you to work on one small block at a time, joining the quilted blocks to make the finished quilt is tedious.

Traditional setting. Following your chosen design, stitch together all the elements (design blocks, plain blocks, dividers, and borders) to make the quilt top. As you did when piecing individual blocks, be very careful to match seams where they join.

Cut both batting and backing according to instructions under "Backing fabric," page 12; baste and quilt the three layers together. (See "Quilting," pages 31–35, for general instructions.) This method, though relatively fast, requires the use of a quilting frame to control tension and smoothness.

Quilt-as-you-go. To put together a quilt by this method, cut batting and backing pieces the same size as the block. With the batting between block and backing, pin and baste the three layers. Quilt to within ½ inch of the raw edges, leaving them open.

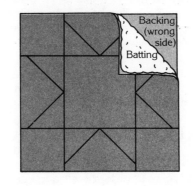
Backing (wrong side)
Batting

When the quilting is completed, place two blocks together, right sides facing and raw edges aligned. Leaving a ¼-inch seam allowance, stitch together the *front pieces only* along one edge. Turn the project over and trim away the excess batting so the edges meet.

Extend the seam allowance out flat on one block, and turn under a ¼-inch seam allowance on the adjacent block; handstitch the two blocks together. Quilt ¼ inch from this seam on each block, stopping ½ inch from the raw edges. Be very careful when working on the back— if you pull the backing too tight, bubbles of extra fabric will appear on the front.

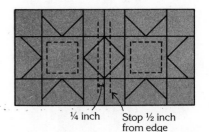
¼ inch
Stop ½ inch from edge

Eventually, as you join blocks, all four edges will be quilted. This quilting secures the batting.

Join blocks to form rows; using the same method, join rows to form the quilt top. Quilt the edge as you go because you'll be working with progressively larger, more unwieldy pieces.

Dividers

Dividers are sometimes called lattices, since these strips create a latticelike effect between blocks. To set off complex design blocks, choose plain dividers; decorative dividers provide contrast for simple blocks.

Traditional dividers. To use dividers on a quilt set in the traditional way, cut short vertical strips the length of the block and the desired width *plus seam allowances*. Stitch these dividers between blocks to form a row.

For horizontal dividers, measure the length of one row, and cut long strips equal to that length. Baste these dividers by hand between rows, and stitch. When joining two rows, mark the junctions of the blocks on the long horizontal dividers to be sure the blocks in one row line up vertically with those in the next row.

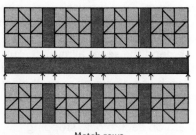

Match rows

Quilt-as-you-go dividers. One method for adding dividers is to sew strips to the right and bottom edges of each completed block before you quilt it. Cut batting and backing to match this new dimension. Blocks in the far right-hand row don't need vertical strips, and the bottom-row blocks don't need horizontal strips.

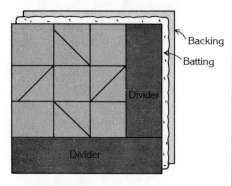

Another method is to cut each divider with matching pieces of batting and backing. Like other blocks, the dividers must be quilted, one edge at a time, as they're joined to blocks. The resulting quilt will have more seams on the back.

Borders

Borders frame a quilt and visually finish the edges. They may be plain strips with decorative quilting or appliqué, or they may be pieced strips. Not all quilts require a border; if you decide a border is right for your quilt, experiment with designs and widths.

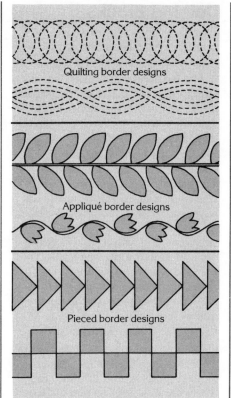

Quilting border designs

Appliqué border designs

Pieced border designs

Generally, the border design should relate to the quilt top in scale and color. If a particular color leaps out of the quilt, contain it by including that color in the border.

Traditional borders. On the lengthwise grain, cut each border strip equal to the length of the appropriate edge plus several more inches, plus twice the desired depth. (Trimming excess length on a border is no problem, but one that's too short is a complete loss.)

If you're piecing the border, first sew border pieces to each other, then join the whole strip to the top. (Adding each border piece separately can make the edges ruffle.) Reverse the direction of your stitching as you add each strip to prevent distortion and stretching.

Before attaching strips, measure and, if necessary, trim quilt top so opposite edges are equal in length and corners are square.

To attach the strips, pin the top and bottom borders to the quilt edges, with right sides facing and raw edges aligned. Make sure the ends of the borders overhang equally on both sides.

For square-corner borders, stitch the top and bottom borders to the quilt top. Trim the borders even with the quilt sides. Open borders and press. Then pin the borders to the side edges, including the previously stitched top and bottom borders; stitch the side borders to the quilt top. Trim the excess length on the side borders, and press.

For mitered corners, stitch the top and bottom borders to the quilt edges, starting and stopping ¼ inch from the edge of the quilt top. Do *not* trim ends. Repeat with the side borders. Press the borders right side up with the ends overlapping; now trim excess from the ends.

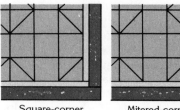

Square-corner border

Mitered-corner border

With right sides facing, pin adjacent borders at the corners; on the wrong side, draw a line from the end of the stitching to the outside edge at a 45-degree angle. Keeping seam allowances free, sew along this diagonal line. Trim the excess to a ¼-inch seam allowance.

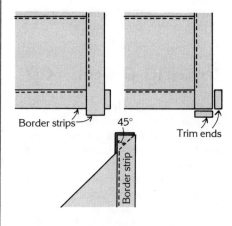

Border strips   45°   Trim ends   Border strip

Quilt-as-you-go borders. The border on a quilt assembled in this manner usually forms the edging. For instructions, see "Quilt-as-you-go edges," page 39.

Quilting

Quilting is the process of stitching together the three layers—top, batting, and backing—into the actual quilt. In years past, it was this stage of quiltmaking that brought people together for stitching and socializing at the quilting bee.

For contemporary quiltmakers who enjoy most the art of combining colors and fabrics in appliqué and patchwork, quilting may seem tedious—a necessary evil. To devoted quilters, it's the icing on the cake—a soothing, rewarding process that transforms a two-dimensional top into a three-dimensional, sculptural textile.

If you study a quilt carefully, you'll see how quilting affects its surface and structure. Quilting gives a finished quilt texture—the loft of the batting creates light areas that contrast with the subtle shadows produced by the lines of stitching.

Quilting also adds durability; many 19th century quilts are still in superb condition because their lines of background quilting are only ⅛ to ½ inch apart.

Quilting designs

You'll want to give as much careful thought to your quilting design as you did to your quilt top. Below are descriptions and illustrations of quilting designs, from simple background quilting to elegant, complex motif quilting. Before you begin stitching, read through this section and make a few sketches of designs you'd like on your quilt.

Outline quilting is lines of quilting just outside the contours of appliqué designs or on either side of seamlines in patchwork.

Around appliqué shapes, outline quilting accentuates the design and anchors the shape more securely to the background, batting, and backing. If there are large open areas

within appliqué pieces, extra quilting lines will prevent shifting of layers.

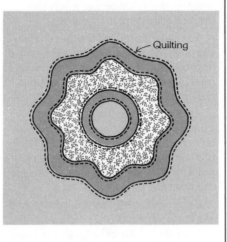

For patchwork, you can place a line of outline quilting on either side of each seamline, or outline only certain areas. On small patchwork areas, you can stitch parallel lines instead of quilting along the seamlines; on large areas, add extra quilting lines within each patch for texture and strength.

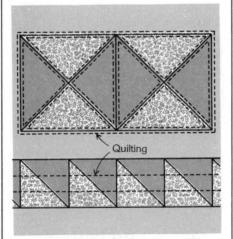

Background quilting—allover quilting filling large areas—compresses the batting and makes the quilted areas recede. This uniform stitching also adds strength and texture to a quilt.

To decide which parts of the quilt top should have background quilting, pin the top to a wall. Step back and squint at the quilt top—the prominent design elements will stand out and the background will recede. Choose a simple quilting design for the background areas, since

they are usually secondary to the appliqué and patchwork areas.

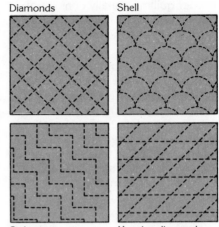

Motif quilting is the intricate, ornamental stitching done in large open areas on a quilt top. Feather wreaths and sprays, hearts, flowers, birds, baskets, lyres, and fans are some traditional examples; in contemporary quilting, abstract designs are popular. Often placed in plain squares and triangles, motif quilting usually repeats designs in the patchwork or appliqué patterns, or in the design of the fabric itself. This type of quilting shows up best when surrounded by background quilting.

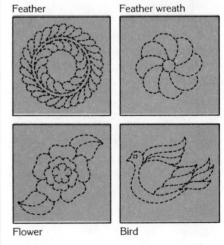

Border quilting finishes and frames the design of the quilt top. When a quilt border is pieced or appliquéd, border quilting usually consists of outline quilting, with background quilting filling in the remainder of the border.

A plain border offers a great opportunity for motif quilting. Border patterns are usually twining repeat patterns that either end at the corners or gracefully turn and continue down the adjoining side. Cables, swags, undulating feathers, and interlocking circles or diamonds are all excellent border motifs.

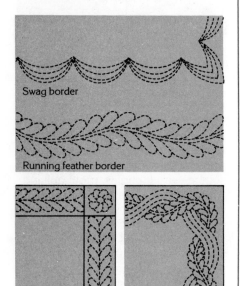

Swag border

Running feather border

A simple and effective border, often seen as a narrow inner border on Amish quilts, consists of large Xs filled with smaller motifs.

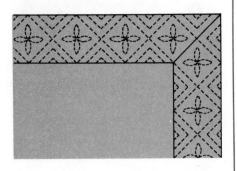

Another simple, elegant border is made of parallel diagonal lines that begin at the corners. Where they meet at the midpoint of each side, opposite lines form chevrons.

To make sure that the border design fills the length of the side and, if appropriate, turns the corners accurately, draw a small version of your design on graph paper.

Another method is to design a quarter of the border on a paper pattern the exact size of the border from the midpoint of one side to the midpoint of the adjoining side, including the corner.

Begin designing at the corner and work out; at each midpoint, you should stop with either one full motif repeat, or exactly half a repeat that is a mirror image of itself. You may have to adjust the design slightly to fit.

If the border is made up of several strips (see page 30), you can either treat each fabric as a separate border and quilt each in a different pattern, or use a design, such as a cable, that crosses and unifies all the borders.

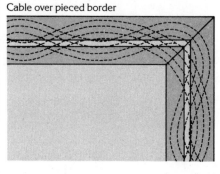

Cable over pieced border

Transferring patterns

It's usually easiest to mark the quilting designs on the quilt top *before* the three layers are assembled. Described below are a number of tools and methods for transferring designs. Whichever technique you choose, work on a firm surface so the marks will be accurate. It's best to mark the entire top so you can see the whole design before you begin quilting and make changes if you wish.

Marking pencils. Before you use any marker, test it on your fabric.

Most—but not all—pencil marks will wash out. To draw directly on the fabric, use a hard lead pencil in a color that will show up on your fabric. On light fabrics, use a regular pencil; try a silver or white pencil, available at art supply stores, on dark fabrics. The pencil should be sharpened to a fine point.

A pencil that shows up well on printed fabrics is an artist's white charcoal pencil. Erasable colored pencils are also excellent.

Templates. Using templates to transfer quilt designs is one simple approach. Cut templates from tagboard. Holding the template firmly in place on the quilt top, draw lightly around the edges; repeat as needed. For overlapping circles, notch the edges of the template where the lines intersect.

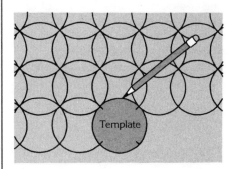

Template

Straightedge. A straightedge makes a good guide for drawing background quilting lines. Straight strips of smooth wood or plastic, cut the width of the space between quilting lines, are timesavers. You can also buy clear plastic rulers in varying widths at art supply stores. Mark along both edges; then shift the straightedge and continue marking until the area is filled with parallel quilting lines. No measuring is necessary. A plastic straightedge you can see through is especially helpful.

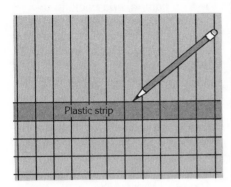

Plastic strip

Light box. Available at art supply stores, a light box is simply a glass-topped box with a light inside. With a light box, or a makeshift light box, you can trace the pattern directly on the quilt top.

Ink your paper pattern so the lines will show through the fabric clearly. Tape your pattern, right side up, on the surface of the light box. Position the area of the quilt to be marked over the pattern and trace the design on the fabric, using an appropriate marking pencil.

If you don't have access to a light box, but do have a glass-top table, you can still use this technique. Simply tape your pattern to the table top, place a small lamp underneath, and you're ready for tracing. A heavy piece of acrylic or glass (taped at the edges for safety) supported by a quilt frame or two small tables will also work as a makeshift light box.

Dressmaker's carbon paper. Transferring with *washable* dressmaker's carbon paper is another possibility. Place the carbon paper *face down* on the area to be marked and pin the pattern to the paper and quilt top. Using a tracing wheel or

sharp pencil, go over the pattern lines slowly and carefully. If a quilting pattern will be traced many times, first transfer the design onto Mylar, a paper-thin, durable plastic available at art supply stores.

Pounce method. Though pounce is no longer available, the method is still an effective way to transfer complex motifs. To use this method, you must make a paper pattern of your quilting design.

Perforate the pattern lines by slowly stitching over them with an unthreaded sewing machine set on the longest stitch. Place the perforated pattern on the quilt top area and shake a small amount of baby powder (powdered cinnamon or nutmeg for light fabrics) over the pattern.

With a powder puff or your fingers, distribute the powder so some of it goes through the holes and leaves a dotted outline on the fabric. Carefully lift off the pattern and, before moving the quilt top, go over the dotted lines with a sharp pencil.

Water-soluble pen. As with marking pencils, you should test any water-soluble pen before touching it to your quilt top. Read package directions carefully.

The advantage of this kind of pen is that you can mark the quilt top after the layers are assembled. The pen leaves a bright mark, visible on most fabrics, that usually comes out after misting or spraying with clear water. (The fabrics must be prewashed, or the water itself may leave spots.) If any faint pen stains remain, spray again to remove completely. Be aware, though, that these marks sometimes reappear and, on some fabrics, are permanent.

Be sure to remove *all* marks before washing the quilt; some detergents will permanently set any leftover marks.

Masking tape. Available in several widths, masking tape is excellent for marking short, straight lines of background quilting, especially in areas like borders. Place a length of tape with one edge where you want a quilting line; quilt along this edge. Since masking tape can damage fabric, quilt immediately after taping and remove the tape as soon as you finish.

Assembling the quilt

Putting together the quilt top, batting, and backing is the last step before you begin quilting in a frame or hoop. Be extra careful when laying out the layers and basting—once they're quilted in, wrinkles are forever.

Basting the quilt. Mark the midpoint of each edge on the backing and quilt top. Lay the backing, wrong side up, on a firm, flat surface. If the backing slips, tape it to the surface. Spread—but do not stretch—the batting on the backing, smoothing out wrinkles carefully. Lay the quilt top, right side up, on the batting and line up the midpoints on the quilt edges with those on the backing.

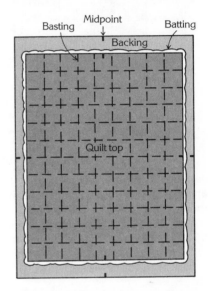

Beginning at the center and working out to the edges, baste the three layers together in lengthwise lines 4 to 6 inches apart; baste crosswise lines, again beginning at the center. The basting lines will intersect, forming a grid that covers the whole quilt.

Frame quilting. To quilt in a frame, you must tack the top and bottom edges of the quilt to the sturdy fabric covering the frame's long poles. Lining up the midpoint of the top or bottom edge of the backing with the midpoint of one pole, baste the backing to the pole, using doubled thread. Support the quilt and the pole on a long table while basting. Then baste the opposite end to the other pole.

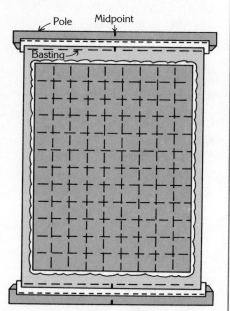

Roll each end toward the center, carefully turning under the batting and top as you go. Place the poles in the quilt frame and adjust so the quilt is taut. At this point, you can secure the sides of the quilt by wrapping and pinning long, narrow strips of fabric or twill tape to the sides.

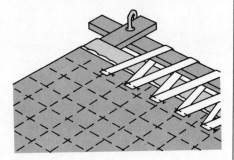

Begin quilting in the center of the quilt and work toward the top or bottom end—any fullness in the quilt top will work out as you quilt. After each section is quilted, unfasten the sides, roll the quilt in one direction to a new area, secure again, and continue quilting. When the first half is done, roll back to the center and work to the other end.

Hoop quilting. Baste the three layers as described, but place the lines of basting even closer together to prevent sagging and shifting. Turn and baste the backing edges to the front to keep the batting from pulling out.

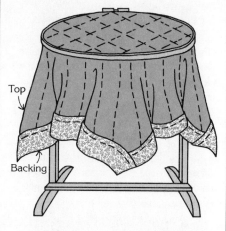

Place the center area of the quilt over the inner hoop, smoothing out any wrinkles or fullness. Put the outer ring over the inner ring and adjust the screw so the quilt is taut, but has enough give to allow comfortable quilting. Quilt from the center out, cutting and removing the basting as you finish each area.

Lap quilting. If you don't have a frame or a hoop, you can still quilt. Baste the three layers as described; since the quilt won't be stretched, it's essential to baste it *thoroughly* to prevent shifting. Bring the backing forward and baste the edges of the backing to the front to keep the batting from pulling out.

Place the quilt on a table with the edges folded up so the quilt is well supported. Allow a small portion of one edge to hang over—this is the edge you'll begin quilting. Or fold the edges up so that an 18-inch area is exposed, and lay the quilt in your lap.

Handquilting

In handquilting, still the most popular method, short running stitches draw the top, batting, and backing together. Knots are buried within the batting, making it almost impossible to see where quilting stops and starts.

The goal of every quilter is to produce small, even stitches that look the same on the top and backing. It takes practice, but it's the rhythmic, repetitive process of stitching that so many quilters enjoy.

Beginning the thread. Thread a quilting needle (see page 8) with an 18-inch length of quilting thread (see page 8); knot the end you've just cut.

Pierce the quilt top ½ inch from where you want to start stitching. Don't go through all layers, but slip the needle horizontally through the batting and bring it up where you want to begin quilting. With a gentle tug, pull the knot through the top layer so the knot lodges in the batting. Begin your quilting stitch just in front of the thread.

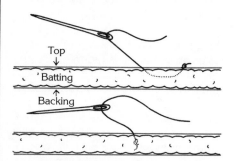

The quilting stitch. Hold the quilting needle between your thumb and forefinger, with the thimble, worn on the middle finger, poised behind the eye of the needle. As you take the first stitch, lodge the eye end of the needle in one of the little thimble grooves; the thimble finger should exert a steady pressure on the needle as you quilt.

Rocking your hand in a slight up and down movement, take three or four stitches through all layers; when you put the needle down through the quilt each time, the point should barely touch the index finger of your hand underneath before coming up to the top again. As you gain experience, your hands will work together and you'll develop a rhythm to your quilting.

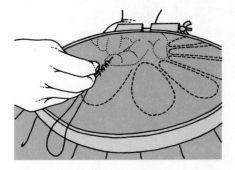

Ending the thread. When you want to end a quilting line, or you run out of thread, make a single looped knot about ¼ inch from the quilt top. Insert the needle into the quilt close to the thread and slip the needle horizontally through the batting and up to the quilt top. Tug gently on the thread and pop the knot into the batting; cut the thread close to the quilt top.

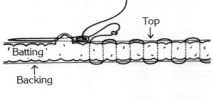

Quilting tips. Here are some useful hints to make your quilting easier and smoother. With a little practice, you'll soon develop your own special techniques for quilting.

• For comfort, start quilting an arm's length away and work toward yourself.

• When quilting a diagonal grid, quilt the design in a zigzag pattern, rather than stitching in long, continuous lines. Zigzag lines reduce the tension on the thread, making the quilting more durable.

• There should be a little give to a quilt stretched on a frame or in a hoop—it's difficult to work on a quilt that's too taut.

• Keep two or three needles threaded and work on close lines in an area for increased efficiency. Quilt with one needle as far as you can; then quilt a parallel line with another needle.

• Avoid unnecessary starts and stops. Instead of knotting and cutting the thread when you come to the end of a design line, skip to a nearby line by running your needle through the batting, and bringing it to the top; continue quilting.

• Curved designs, such as feathers, are often difficult to quilt because the lines change direction. Develop a pattern for quilting these shapes; stitch as far as is comfortable, then skip to another line that goes in the same direction.

Trapunto

Trapunto, or Italian quilting, refers to the technique of outlining and stuffing motifs for a padded, sculptural effect. Relatively small designs with curved lines, such as flowers, feath-

ers, and leaves, lend themselves to this technique.

Many beautiful antique quilts were made by this painstaking method. With a coarse fabric for backing, the designs were first outlined with quilting. Then, working from the back, the quiltmaker gently spread the threads in the area to be stuffed and inserted bits of batting until the area was raised. The holes were then worked closed. This technique required a great deal of patience and time.

You can achieve the same results with a short-cut trapunto method.

Stitching the designs. Transfer the quilting design to the top piece (see pages 32–33). Cut a backing piece from thin fabric, such as voile or lightweight muslin; with wrong sides facing, baste the top and backing pieces together. Note that no batting is used between the two layers. Outline the design in small, even quilting stitches.

Stuffing the designs. Working from the back, cut a small slit within a design area enclosed by quilting. *Be sure to cut only the backing fabric, not the top.* Using a blunt needle or crochet hook, insert a small amount of batting between the layers. Continue stuffing until the motif is smooth and puffy. Don't overstuff, or the area will pucker and the design will be distorted. Fill *all* the motifs before you close each opening with a whipstitch so you can compare the consistency of the stuffing.

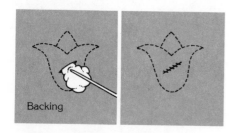
Backing

Corded quilting

You can stuff designs by running lengths of preshrunk cotton or synthetic yarn between the top and backing. To prepare and quilt the two pieces, see "Stitching the designs," above.

Stuffing the designs. Use a blunt tapestry needle threaded with a double length of yarn. Working from the back, carefully insert the needle between the layers near one end of the design. Work the needle to the other end of the design and bring it out again inside the stitching. Pull the yarn through and trim close to the fabric, both at the start and finish; work the ends of yarn into the holes. Repeat this process to fill the motif.

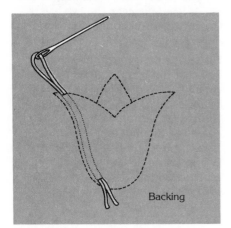
Backing

Linear designs. To stuff linear motifs such as vines and monograms, you must first quilt two parallel lines. Then thread a blunt tapestry needle with a single or double length of yarn. Working from the back, carefully insert the needle between the two layers at the beginning of the design.

Run the needle between the quilting lines, gathering the fabric as you go. Bring the needle out where the design turns, insert the needle again, and continue, leaving a little extra yarn out at each turn to prevent puckering. At the start and finish, trim the ends of the yarn close to the fabric, and work the ends into the holes.

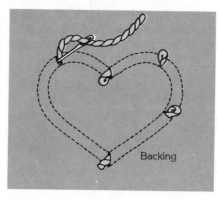
Backing

Machine quilting

Though purists scoff at anything but handquilting, there are times when quilting with a sewing machine is appropriate—and very successful, If you value completing a project over using a traditional method, this may be your technique.

It takes practice to achieve smooth, even machine quilting, but the initial investment may be well worth the time you save, especially if you're making several projects.

To quilt by machine or not? Small projects, such as pot holders and crib quilts, are excellent candidates for machine quilting. The use intended for them may not justify the time needed for handquilting; also, they're small enough to maneuver easily under a sewing machine. Quilt-as-you-go projects (see pages 29 and 30) also lend themselves to machine quilting.

Full-size quilts are another matter. They can be quilted by machine, but most quiltmakers find that the size and weight of a large quilt make it difficult to handle on a machine, particularly if there's a great deal of pivoting.

In addition to project size, consider the complexity of your designs when choosing between machine and handquilting. It's frustrating and time-consuming to machine quilt intricate appliqué designs that require a lot of turning.

Machine quilting works best on patchwork, where you can quilt in straight lines ¼ inch from the seamlines. Allover grid patterns are also easily stitched by machine.

If you do decide to quilt by machine, the following procedures will make your work go faster and more smoothly.

Assembling the quilt. Baste the quilt top, batting, and backing together as you would for traditional quilting (see page 33). Remember to allow extra fabric at all edges if you plan a self-finished edge (see pages 37–38). Because there's so much pressure on the quilt when you machine stitch, thorough basting is critical to prevent bunching.

Following your machine instruction booklet, loosen the tension and pressure slightly, and set the stitch length for 8 to 10 stitches per inch. Use a regular presser foot and a small-hole throat plate; a special quilting guide, available for most machines, makes it easier to stitch parallel lines.

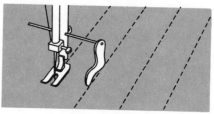
Quilting guide

Be sure to practice machine quilting on a basted sample of your top, batting, and backing until you're satisfied with the results.

Before you begin stitching the quilt, roll opposite edges toward the center, keeping an 18-inch area open to work on. On the left side of the machine, set up a table to support the bulk and weight of your work.

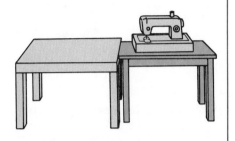

A quilting plan. A carefully thought-out sequence of quilting will save many time-consuming starts and stops. Try to stitch continuous lines that pivot at the edges. A simplified quilting plan that uses only two continuous lines is shown below. If you prefer a more complex background grid pattern, you can add lines to this basic design.

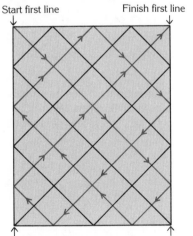

Start first line   Finish first line

Start second line   Finish second line

Ending threads. With quilting that extends to the edges, you don't need to finish off the thread ends. But if you start and stop in the middle of the quilt, leave about 3 inches of both the top and bobbin threads. Thread a needle with the top thread and run the needle through the batting, bringing the needle up again to the top. Trim the thread end close to the quilt. Repeat on the back with the bobbin thread.

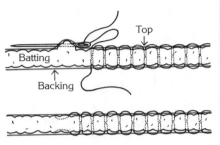

Top

Batting

Backing

Tied quilting

Tying is a simple way of holding together the three layers of a quilt without quilting. Often used for comforters and children's quilts, tying allows you to use the heavy or double polyester batting that's usually too thick for handquilting. (Don't use cotton batting in a tied quilt, since it shifts too easily.) Because the batting isn't compressed when you tie a quilt, the loft remains high, providing more insulation and warmth.

Basting and marking the quilt. Assemble the three layers as you would for handquilting (see page 33). If the quilt is small, or you're in a hurry, you can pin rather than baste the layers together.

Decide how far apart to place the ties. On a patchwork quilt top, you'll want to tie the corners of each block and perhaps several spots within each block—preferably on seamlines. Whatever the top design, the ties should fall no farther than 6 inches apart.

Using a suitable marking pencil (see pages 32 and 33), mark the points to be tied.

Tying the knot. The most typical tie is the square knot. Use a long needle threaded with a double length of yarn or perle cotton.

With the quilt on a flat surface, begin tying along one edge. Insert the needle from the top to the back, drawing the yarn through and leaving a 2-inch tail on top. (Start on the back if you don't want the knots to show on the quilt top.) Bring the needle back up to the top and cut the yarn so another 2-inch tail remains. Tie the ends in a square knot as shown—left over right, then right over left. Trim the ends to the desired length.

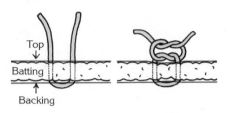

Top

Batting

Backing

Once you've tied as far as you can comfortably reach, roll the finished edge and continue working until the entire quilt is tied. Finish the edges (see below).

Finishing the edges

Because the edges of a quilt receive so much wear, you'll want to finish them as securely as possible. Before you choose the method you want to use, consider how much use your quilt will get. Though a self-finished edge—folding the backing to the front and stitching it down—is simplest, you'll achieve greatest durability by adding a separate binding.

Self-finished edges

One popular technique is to fold a narrow band of excess backing to the quilt front to form a binding. Of course, you must provide in advance for this finished edge by cutting the backing fabric larger than the quilt top measurement. The backing should extend beyond the quilt top a distance equal to the desired finished binding width, plus a seam allowance. Also, you'll want to choose a backing fabric that harmonizes with the quilt top.

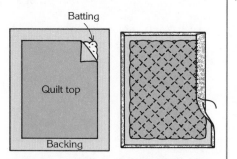

Before folding the backing forward, measure and trim all edges to the proper width. Bring the backing over the quilt top, turn under the seam allowance, and hand or machine stitch. To form miters at the corners, fold each corner point forward so the diagonal fold is directly over the corner point of the quilt top. Trim the point, then fold straight edges forward to form a miter.

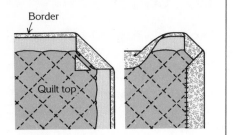

You can also turn excess quilt top fabric to the back of the quilt. You'll want to handstitch the binding down because machine stitching will show on the top of the quilt.

For a reversible quilt, simply slipstitch the quilt top and backing together at the edges. To use this closure, quilt only to within ½ inch from all sides so you can turn under the top and backing.

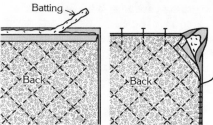

Trim the quilt top and backing; trim the batting ¼ inch shorter than the top and backing. Fold the top over the batting; then fold the backing under ¼ inch and slipstitch the edges together.

Added edges

If you don't want to use the backing for an edging, or if you need a more durable edge, add a separate binding. Straight strips work well if the borders are straight; bias binding is necessary if the quilt top is curved or if you don't have enough fabric for straight strips.

Separate bias strips. This method of adding separate edging is simple, but if you need many strips, it's very time-consuming.

1 Fold a corner of fabric so selvage is aligned with crosswise cut; press bias fold and cut fabric along fold.

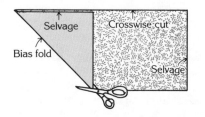

2 Using diagonal cut as a guideline, measure and mark strips parallel to cut. Stop when bottom edge of strip is no longer on crosswise cut. (Strips are easiest to join when their ends are on crosswise grain of fabric.) Cut along lines.

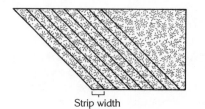

Strip width

3 With right sides facing, place 2 strips at a right angle, offset slightly as shown, and stitch together, leaving ¼-inch seam allowance; press seam open. Sew strips together to make a continuous strip.

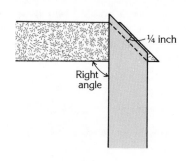

Continuous bias casing. Cutting continuous bias casing looks complex, but it's very efficient in terms of fabric and effort.

1 Fold a square of fabric in half diagonally; press fold and cut fabric along fold.

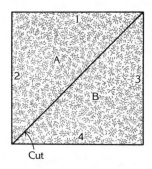

2 Reposition triangles as shown to form a parallelogram. With right sides facing, stitch triangles together,

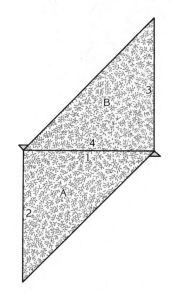

leaving a ¼-inch seam allowance. Press seam open.

3 Using top diagonal cut as a guideline, measure and mark strips parallel to cut.

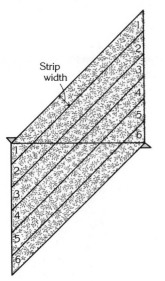

Strip width

4 With right sides facing and edges mismatched as shown, stitch edges together to form tube.

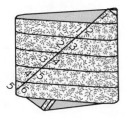

5 Starting at top, cut tube along lines to form a continuous bias strip.

Attaching strips. To attach binding strips to a quilt, pin together the quilt top, batting, and backing at the edges and machine baste through all layers ⅛ inch from the quilt top edge. Trim the batting and backing so they're even with the quilt top.

Fold the binding strips in half lengthwise, with right sides out; press the folds.

If the final sewing is done by hand, place a binding strip along one edge of the quilt top, with raw edges aligned. Machine stitch ¼ inch from the edge. Repeat on the opposite edge of the quilt. Fold the strips to the back and handstitch to conceal the machine stitching.

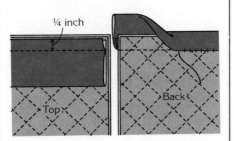

¼ inch

Top   Back

Repeat this procedure on the other two edges so the binding strips overlap the ends of the first two strips at the corners.

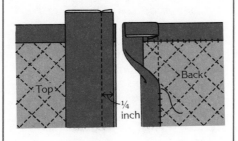

Top   Back
¼ inch

If the final stitching is done by machine, follow these same steps, but sew the binding to the backing first so the final topstitching will appear on the quilt top.

Quilt-as-you-go edges

In the quilt-as-you-go method, you add edges in the same way that you attach dividers to blocks (see page 30). The front and back edges are one piece of fabric folded in half lengthwise. The width of the strips should equal twice the desired *finished* edge width, plus seam al-

lowances; the length of each strip should equal the length of the appropriate edge (including the borders you've just added), plus several inches for leeway.

With right sides out, fold each edge strip in half lengthwise and press the fold. Baste the batting to the wrong side of half the edge strip.

Attach the edges to the quilt following the quilt-as-you-go procedure. Quilt, leaving the overlapping corners free.

To miter each corner, trim the excess batting and fabric on the top and bottom (horizontal) borders even with the outside fold of the side (vertical) edge. Open up the side edge and trim the batting so it overlaps the top or bottom batting by ¼ inch; trim the fabric so it extends 1 inch beyond the outside fold of the top or bottom edge.

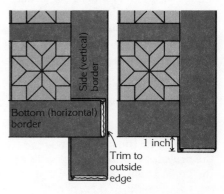

Side (vertical) border

Bottom (horizontal) border

Trim to outside edge

1 inch

Fold under this fabric extension so it's even with the top or bottom edge; pin the two edges together at the corner. Turn under the front edge at a 45-degree angle to form a miter. Finger-press, trim away excess fabric to ¼ inch, and stitch closed. Repeat on the back edge.

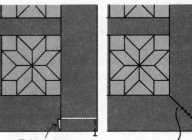

Fold under seam allowance

Mitered corner

Patchwork & Quilting Projects

Say "quilts" and most people envision bed covers of print patchwork or floral appliqué. As the next 30 pages illustrate, the techniques for patchwork, appliqué, and quilting need not be confined to large quilt-making projects. You may, indeed, choose to make a large quilt; this chapter includes both a traditional favorite, the Double Irish Chain, and a quick-to-make tied quilt based on the Amish Roman Stripe design.

If you're not quite ready to take on a full-size quilt, try one of our smaller projects—a pair of handsome patchwork pillows, a stunning holiday tablecloth, a graphic wall hanging, or a delightful child's string vest.

These are contemporary projects, made recently, yet they reflect the wide—and exciting—range of traditional quiltmaking designs. As you look through the photos and read the project introductions, you'll see the lasting influence of Amish quilts, log cabin quilts, and crazy quilts. Some projects, such as the Baskets Wall Hanging and the Castle Wall Placemats, interpret popular traditional patterns in new ways. Others, like the Appliquéd Crib Quilt, are new designs.

Before you tackle any of these projects, read the list of materials and instructions carefully and try to visualize how the project goes together. Refer to the techniques chapter; it will give you a feeling for the complexity and scope of the project. Once you understand what's involved, you'll be able to decide if it's the right one for you.

Bars and Shadows

Simple and stunning, Amish designs possess a vitality and richness unrivaled in the world of quilting. Here, the designer chose subtle fabrics and geometric shapes to translate two well-known Amish quilt designs, Bars and Shadows, into easy-to-make pillows. If you're new to patchwork, this pair makes an ideal first project. Design: Glendora Hutson.

Gather together . . .

For one *Bars* pillow 15 inches square:
½ yard olive green fabric
⅛ yard *each* navy, magenta, and beige fabrics
2 yards welt
16-inch (actual size) square pillow form
Thread

For one *Shadows* pillow 15 inches square:
⅝ yard navy fabric
¼ yard beige fabric
⅛ yard *each* plum, magenta, peacock blue, and forest green fabrics for stripes
2 yards welt
16-inch (actual size) square pillow form
1 sheet acetate (see page 9)
Craft knife (see page 9)
Metal ruler

Piecing Bars pillow

Note: Preshrink and press fabrics. Piece pillow tops using ¼-inch seam allowance; stitch outside pillow edges using ½-inch seam allowance.

1 See diagram, above right, for arrangement and size of pieces for Bars design. Measure and mark pieces on appropriate fabrics, placing rectangular pieces on lengthwise

grain where possible. *Add ¼-inch seam allowance to all edges* of each piece, plus an *extra* ¼ inch to outside pillow edges. Cut pieces.

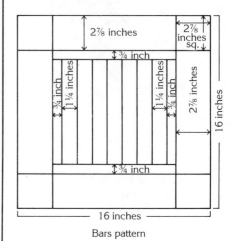

Bars pattern

2 With right sides facing, stitch center bars together; press seams in one direction. Stitch shorter navy strips to magenta bars; press seams, and all seams that follow, toward edges. Attach longer navy strips to remaining sides.

3 With right sides facing, stitch two olive green border strips to side edges of patchwork. Stitch navy squares to ends of remaining olive strips. Matching seamlines, stitch olive strips with squares to top and bottom edges of patchwork.

4 To finish pillow, see "Making the pillows," opposite.

Piecing Shadows pillow

1 See diagram, above right, for arrangement of pieces for Shadows design. On *each* fabric except beige, measure and mark a strip 1¼ by 21 inches. Cut strips.

With right sides facing, stitch strips together to form striped piece 4¼ by 21 inches. Press seams in one direction.

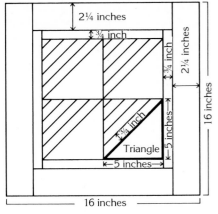

2¼ inches
¾ inch
2¼ inches
2¼ inches
¾ inch
16 inches
Triangle
5 inches
5 inches
16 inches

Shadows pattern

2 Cut triangular acetate template (see pages 15–16) to size shown on diagram above, *making sure to add ¼-inch seam allowance to all edges.*

Using template, mark four triangles on striped piece. Cut triangles. Using template, mark and cut four triangles from beige fabric.

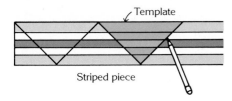

Template

Striped piece

3 With right sides facing, stitch long edges of striped and beige triangles together to form four squares. Press seams toward striped triangles.

4 Arrange squares as shown in photo. With right sides facing and corners matching, stitch squares together to form large square.

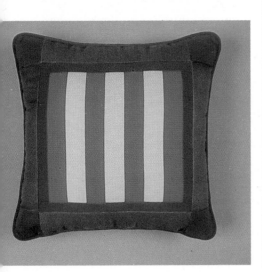

5 On remaining magenta fabric, measure and mark four inner border strips: two 1¼ by 12 inches, and two 1¼ by 10½ inches. Cut strips.

On navy fabric, measure and mark four outside border strips: two 3 by 12 inches, and two 3 by 17 inches. Cut strips.

6 With right sides facing, stitch shorter magenta border strips to opposite sides of square; press these seams, and all seams that follow, toward edges. Stitch longer magenta strips to remaining sides. In same manner, attach navy border strips.

Making the pillows

1 On olive fabric for Bars pillow and navy fabric for Shadows pillow, measure and mark one 17-inch square for pillow bottom. Cut square.

2 Attach zipper foot. Starting at midpoint of any edge, baste welt to pillow top, using ½-inch seam allowance and leaving first 1½ inches of welt free. Stop stitching 1½ inches from corner, and make three diagonal cuts into welt seam allowance *almost* to stitching. Gently curve welt around corner.

3 To join welt ends, continue sewing to within 1 inch of first welt end. Stop stitching, leaving needle in fabric. Cut off welt so it overlaps first welt end by 1½ inches. Pull out and cut off ¾ inch of cord from each welt end. Cross empty casings and finish basting.

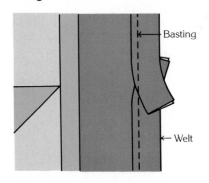

← Basting

← Welt

4 With right sides facing and raw edges aligned, pin pillow top and bottom pieces together. With welted piece on top, stitch around pillow between welt stitching and cord, leaving most of one side open to insert pillow form. Clip corners.

5 Turn pillow right side out. If necessary, press edges. Insert pillow form, pin open edge, and handstitch closed.

Christmas Log Cabin Tablecloth

Symbolic of the warmth and hospitality of early American family life, the log cabin design is a particularly appropriate pattern for this festive holiday tablecloth. It combines compatible prints in reds and greens for spiraling blocks. Arrange the completed blocks on point, as shown, or play with other possibilities for your own setting variation. Design: Nancy Shelby.

Gather together . . .

For 60-inch-square tablecloth:
- 1 yard dark green print fabric (A), 45 inches wide
- ¾ yard medium green print fabric (B)
- ½ yard light green print fabric (C)
- ¼ yard light red print fabric (D)
- ½ yard medium red print fabric (E)
- ⅞ yard dark red print fabric (F)
- ⅝ yard white print fabric (G)
- 7¼ yards 5-inch-wide border print trim or 1¼ yards print fabric for border
- 3½ yards white fabric for lining
  Thread
- 1 sheet acetate (see page 9)
  Craft knife (see page 9)
  Metal ruler
  Graph paper

Piecing the patchwork

Note: Preshrink and press fabrics.

1 See "Log cabin quilt construction," page 19, to fold, measure, mark, and cut all print fabrics except white print (G) into 2-inch-wide strips. Cut 13 strips from fabric A, nine strips from B, four strips from C, two strips from D, six strips from E, and 12 strips from F. Cut light red strips (D) into 25 center squares, each 2 inches.

2 To piece 25 log cabin blocks using railroading method, see "A quilted log cabin quilt," page 20. For each block, begin with center square (D) and light green logs (C); following diagram above right, stitch subsequent logs in counterclockwise direction. Finished block should measure 9½ inches square.

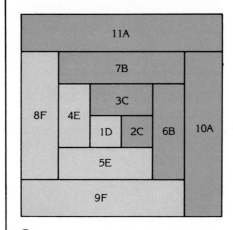

3 To make patterns for large (edge) and small (corner) triangles, draw a 9-inch square on graph paper, and divide as shown below. *Add ¼-inch seam allowance to all edges.* See "Cutting a template," pages 15–16, to cut templates from patterns.

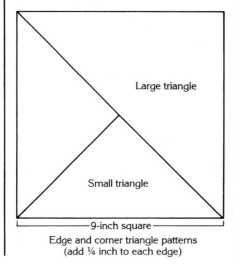

Edge and corner triangle patterns
(add ¼ inch to each edge)

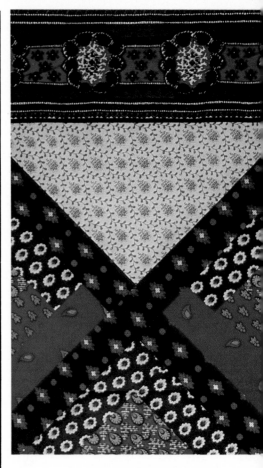

4 On white print (G), measure and mark four small triangles and 12 large triangles. Cut pieces.

5 Begin piecing at top corner. With right sides facing and raw edges aligned, pin and stitch small triangle to top edge of block, as shown below. Press seam, and all seams that follow, toward edge. Stitch large triangles to side edges of block in same manner to make first row.

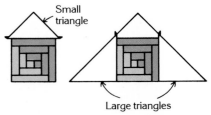

For second row, stitch together three blocks, following patchwork diagram on facing page; attach large triangles to side edges of first and third blocks to complete row. Continue stitching blocks and triangles together for subsequent rows; stitch rows together to complete patchwork.

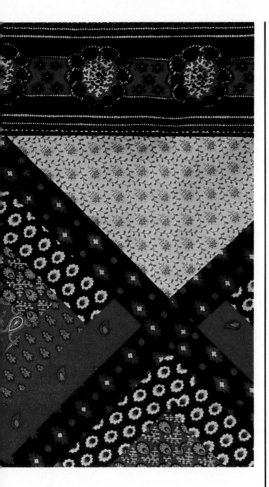

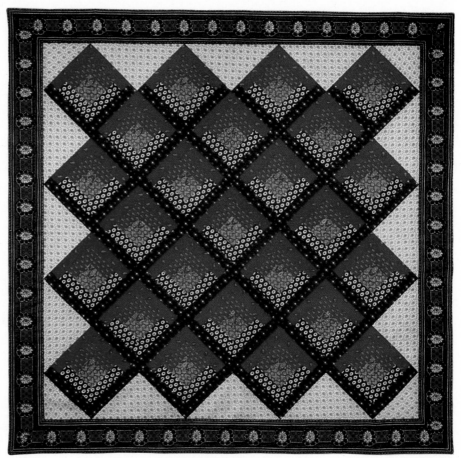

6 On border trim, measure and mark four strips, each 65 inches long. Cut strips. (If not using border print trim, cut and piece 5-inch-wide strips of print border fabric to make four strips, each 65 inches long.) See "Borders," page 30, to attach borders to tablecloth top and to miter corners. Press tablecloth carefully.

Lining the tablecloth

1 Cut lining fabric into two lengths, each 1¾ yards. With right sides facing, sew pieces together along selvage edges, using ⅝-*inch seam allowance*. Cut off selvages and press seam open.

2 Lay lining, right side up, on floor or large work surface; smooth out wrinkles. Lay tablecloth, right side down, over lining and pin together at edges. Stitch around edge, using ¼-inch seam allowance and leaving 12 inches open on one edge. Turn right side out and press.

3 Pin open edge and handstitch closed. Topstitch 1 inch from edges.

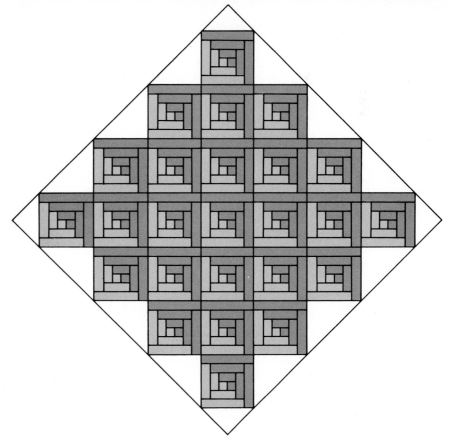

Castle Wall Placemats

Looking as pretty as plates themselves, these pieced placemats are almost too lovely to cover up. One of the more complex patchwork patterns, Castle Wall lends itself beautifully to a mélange of solid, striped, and printed fabrics. Design: Victoria Sears.

Gather together . . .

For set of four placements:
1 yard dark green solid fabric
¾ yard dark green print fabric (allow more if fabric has stripes or motifs that must be matched)
⅞ yard light green solid fabric
¼ yard light green print fabric
1 yard solid fabric for backing
1 yard batting
    Thread to match backing
1 sheet acetate (see page 9)
    Craft knife (see page 9)
    Metal ruler

Piecing the placemats

Note: Preshrink and press fabrics. Directions are for one placemat. Complete each placemat individually, or repeat each step four times before starting the next step.

1 Carefully trace full-size pattern pieces shown at far right. To make patterns, *add ¼-inch seam allowance to all edges.* See "Cutting a template," pages 15–16, to cut templates. Label each template.

2 Measure, mark, and cut following pieces in fabrics specified: template 1—from light green solid, 16 pieces; template 2—from dark green print, 32 pieces; template 3—from light green print, 32 pieces; template 4—from dark green solid, 32 pieces; and template 5—from dark green print, 32 pieces.

3 For piecing hints, see "Sewing," pages 16–17.

With right sides facing and raw edges aligned, stitch pairs of piece 5 together, using ¼-inch seam allowance. Press seams open and trim extending points. Join two pairs to

make half of center octagon; repeat with remaining pairs; join halves to form center unit A.

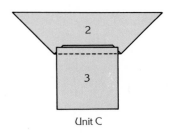

4 Join pieces 1, 2, and 3 to form unit B; press seams toward corner triangle. Repeat for four units.

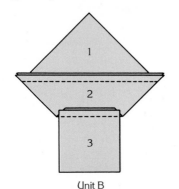

Unit B

5 Form unit C by joining pieces 2 and 3 as shown; repeat to make a total of four units.

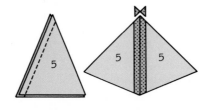

Unit C

6 Starting ¼ inch in from edge, stitch piece 4 to one edge of piece 2 as shown above, next column; stop stitching ¼ inch from other edge. With needle in fabric, raise presser foot, pivot work, and continue stitching to join second edge of piece 4 to edges of piece 3. Stop ¼ inch from edge. Press seams away from piece 4. Trim extending points. Stitch another piece 4 to other side of unit C, forming unit D. Repeat to make a total of four units.

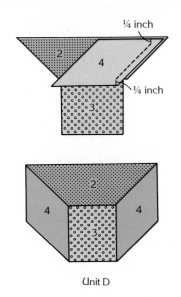

¼ inch

¼ inch

Unit D

7 Attach unit B to unit D, stitching with piece 4 on top and pivoting at corner as before. Stop ¼ inch from edge. Press seam away from piece 4. Join remaining units B and D until you have formed entire outside ring.

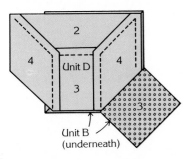

Unit D

Unit B
(underneath)

8 Set center unit A into outside piece, sewing each edge of octagon to a square in outside ring. Start and stop seams ¼ inch from each edge. Press seams toward center. Square should measure 12 inches; trim edges, if necessary.

Making the placemats

1 From dark green solid, measure and mark 16 crosswise strips 3 by 22 inches for borders; from light green solid, measure and mark 16 strips 2 by 22 inches for binding. Cut strips.

2 With right sides facing and raw edges aligned, pin dark green border strips to patchwork square, matching midpoints on edges. Stitch, starting and stopping ¼ inch from edges. To miter corners, see "Borders," page 30. *Do not* trim excess off border strips—as cut, they're the proper length.

3 Press placemat top carefully. Measure, mark, and cut batting and backing pieces to equal dimensions of placemat top.

4 Baste three layers together and machine quilt (see pages 36–37) along lines shown in quilting pattern at right.

5 To finish edges with light green binding strips, see "Attaching strips," page 39, disregarding last paragraph.

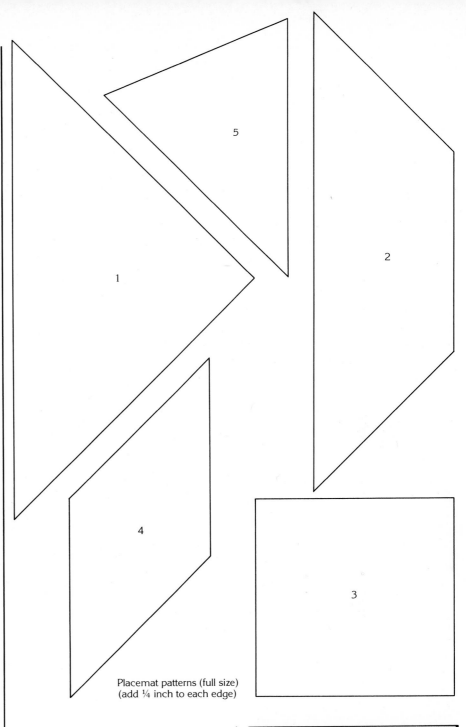

Placemat patterns (full size)
(add ¼ inch to each edge)

Quilting pattern

Appliquéd Crib Quilt

Bouquets of violets greet an April baby on this delicate appliquéd and embroidered crib quilt. Splash violets across your quilt just like this one, or use the flower for the month of the baby's birth. Constructed by the quilt-as-you-go method, the quilt has a backing of purple print dividers crisscrossing light print blocks. Design: Phyllis Dunstan.

Gather together . . .

For quilt 44 by 58 inches:
3¼ yards light floral print fabric for blocks and outside borders
1½ yards dark purple print fabric for dividers and outside corners
1⅛ yards small green gingham fabric for borders
¼ yard lavender fabric for violets
¼ yard green fabric for leaves
2 yards batting, 45 inches wide
½ yard *each* iron-on interfacing and fusible web
    Thread, green and lavender machine embroidery and white quilting
    Embroidery floss, green and yellow
    Perle cotton, green

Appliquéing the blocks

Note: Preshrink and press fabrics.

1 To enlarge violets design shown above to fit 10-inch square, see "Enlarging designs," page 22. "Widest part of design" mentioned in step 1 should be *outside edges* of this block, not flower edges. From enlarged pattern, cut flower and leaf pieces.

    Apply half of iron-on interfacing to wrong side of lavender fabric and half to wrong side of green fabric. Cut lavender flower and green leaf pieces for six blocks according to instructions under "Preparations," page 23. *Do not* add seam allowance to edges.

2 On light print fabric, measure and mark six background blocks 10¾ inches square for quilt top, and six backing blocks 12½ inches square; place blocks in pairs near selvage

10 inches

Quilting lines

Violets appliqué pattern

edge of fabric. (You'll need remaining fabric for cutting long border strips.) Cut blocks. Also cut six 12-inch squares of batting.

3 Using patterns, cut a piece of matching fusible web for each flower and leaf. Following manufacturer's instructions for fusible web, fuse leaves—except leaf 5—to each background block; fuse flowers, then leaf 5.

4 Thread machine with green embroidery thread and set for satin stitch (closely spaced zigzag stitch). On each background block, appliqué leaves; change to lavender thread and appliqué flowers. (Insert a piece of typing paper under block to help prevent puckering.) Press blocks.

5 With green perle cotton, embroider stems using a stem stitch. With all six strands of green embroidery floss, embroider leaf veins and flower details using a stem stitch; add yellow French knots made from embroidery floss to violet centers. Trim each block to 10½ inches square.

6 On green gingham, measure and mark 24 narrow border strips 1½ by 12½ inches. Cut strips. With right sides facing and raw edges aligned, stitch borders to top and bottom edges of each block, using ¼-inch seam allowance. Press seams toward borders; trim ends even with edges of block. Attach narrow border strips to side edges of block, including top and bottom borders. Press seams toward borders.

7 For each block, pin and baste backing, batting, and appliquéd squares together. Following quilting lines shown on pattern, handquilt (see pages 34–35) around bouquets and outside edges.

Joining blocks and rows

1 On dark purple print, measure and mark 26 divider strips 3½ inches wide and equal to length of edge of quilted block. Cut strips. Cut 17 strips of batting 3 inches wide and equal to length of divider strips.

(Continued on next page)

2 With right sides facing, sandwich one side edge of quilted block between two divider strips; stitch through all thicknesses, using ¼-inch seam allowance.

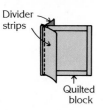

3 Join *top divider strip only* to side edge of *second* quilted block, leaving back divider strip free. Mark large diamond quilting pattern (see pages 32–33) on top strip. *Do not* extend pattern into ¼-inch seam allowance at top and bottom of strip.

4 Working from back, slip strip of batting between top and back divider strips. Turn under raw edge of back divider strip ¼ inch and, using invisible hemming stitch (see page 24), handstitch to back of second block. Baste three layers together and quilt. In same manner, add strips to outside edges of first and second blocks to make first row. Repeat for two more rows.

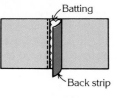

5 To assemble horizontal dividers, cut twelve 3½-inch squares of light floral print. Stitch a square between two dark purple divider strips and a square to end of each strip as shown above, next column. Adjust seams, if necessary, so squares will line up with dark purple vertical dividers.

For backing, cut four long dark purple strips equal to width and length of horizontal dividers just pieced. From batting, cut four 3-inch-wide strips equal to length of dividers. Attach dividers to top edge of first row, between rows, and to bottom edge of third row in manner described above.

Slip strips of batting between dividers; baste and quilt. Trim edges so quilt is square.

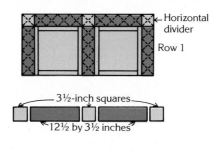

Adding borders and edges

Note: Cut side borders on lengthwise grain of fabric, and cut top and bottom borders on crosswise grain.

1 For side borders, measure and mark two light floral border strips 5 inches wide and equal to length of side edge of quilt plus 1 inch (fabric draws up a little when you quilt). On gingham, measure and mark two strips 1½ inches wide and equal to length of floral border strips. Cut strips. Stitch each gingham strip to a floral strip to make 6-inch-wide border strip. Press seams toward gingham strips. Mark quilting design of parallel lines 1½ inches apart running crosswise to long edge of border.

For backing borders, cut two light floral strips 6 inches wide and equal to length of quilt top side borders. Also cut two strips of batting 7¾ inches wide and equal to length of side borders.

2 Attach top and backing borders to side edges of quilt (let each strip extend ½ inch beyond edge of quilt on each end). Slip strips of batting between borders, baste, and quilt (2 inches of batting will extend beyond outside edges).

3 For top and bottom borders, measure, mark, and cut strips and squares as follows: two light floral strips 5 by 33½ inches, four gingham strips 5 by 1½ inches, and four dark purple 5-inch squares.

Using diagram above, next column, as a guide, stitch border strips and squares together, adjusting seams so gingham strips are aligned with vertical gingham strips on side borders. Press seams toward gingham.

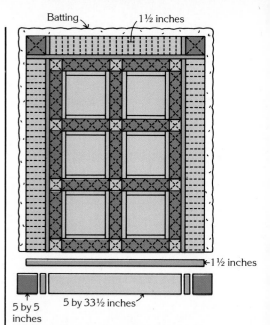

Measure, mark, and cut two gingham strips 1½ inches wide and equal to length of top and bottom borders. Stitch one gingham strip to each border strip to make 6-inch-wide border. Press seams toward gingham.

For backing borders, measure, mark, and cut two light floral strips 6 inches wide and equal to length of pieced borders. Also cut two strips of batting 7¾ inches wide and 2¼ inches longer *on each end* than borders.

4 Attach borders to top and bottom edges; insert batting, baste, and quilt (2 inches of batting will extend beyond edges).

5 From gingham, measure, mark, and cut four 3½-inch-wide edge strips, two equal to length of top and bottom edges, and two equal to length of side edge plus 5 inches (you may have to piece strips).

6 Working from back, stitch one shorter gingham strip to top edge and one to bottom edge, with right sides together and raw edges aligned. Fold each strip forward to quilt top, folding extending batting in half. Turn under ¼ inch on raw edge, and pin to quilt top. Topstitch through all layers close to turned-under edge. Trim ends of edges.

7 Attach side strips in same manner, but fold raw ends of each edge piece to inside before folding forward.

Plain Crib Quilt

What could be simpler? Four floral borders surround a center piece on this machine-stitched crib quilt. The term "plain quilt" comes from Amish quilts that didn't have the geometric pieces characteristic of quilts. On plain quilts, the emphasis was on color and elaborate quilting.

You can assemble and quilt this project quickly by machine, or follow the Amish tradition of decorating simple piecework with intricate handquilting. Design: Nancy Shelby.

Gather together . . .

For quilt 36 by 54 inches:
2¼ yards pink print fabric, 45 inches wide
1⅜ yards white print fabric
½ yard green print fabric
1 yard batting, 54 inches wide
    Thread
    Metal ruler
    Yardstick
    Masking tape

Piecing the top

Note: Preshrink and press fabrics.

1 On pink print, measure and mark one lengthwise piece 37 by 55 inches for backing, and one crosswise piece 19 by 37 inches for top center. On remaining areas, measure and mark two lengthwise border strips 3 by 51 inches, and two crosswise border strips 3 by 37 inches. Cut pieces. Using pencil, mark a rectangle 6 by 24 inches on top center piece.

On white print, measure and mark eight lengthwise strips: two 3 by 47 inches, two 3 by 37 inches, two 3 by 33 inches, and two 3 by 23 inches. Cut strips.

On green print, measure and mark four crosswise strips: two 4 by 41 inches, and two 4 by 29 inches. Cut strips.

2 With right sides facing and raw edges aligned, pin 37-inch-long white print strips to long edges of top center piece. Stitch, using ½-inch seam allowance. Press seams, and all seams that follow, toward borders. Attach 23-inch-long white strips to short edges of center piece.

Always starting with long strips, attach green borders, remaining white borders, and pink borders. Press pieced top.

Finishing the quilt

1 Lay batting on floor or table. Over it, place backing, *right side up*, and quilt top, *right side down.* Pin layers together at edges; trim excess batting.

2 Stitch around edges, using ½-inch seam allowance and leaving most of one short edge open; trim corners. Turn right side out and press lightly. Pin open edge closed.

3 With masking tape, secure quilt to floor or table. Pin layers together along marked center lines and along border seamlines. Remove tape.

4 Machine quilt (see pages 36–37) along center lines and seamlines. Handstitch open edge closed.

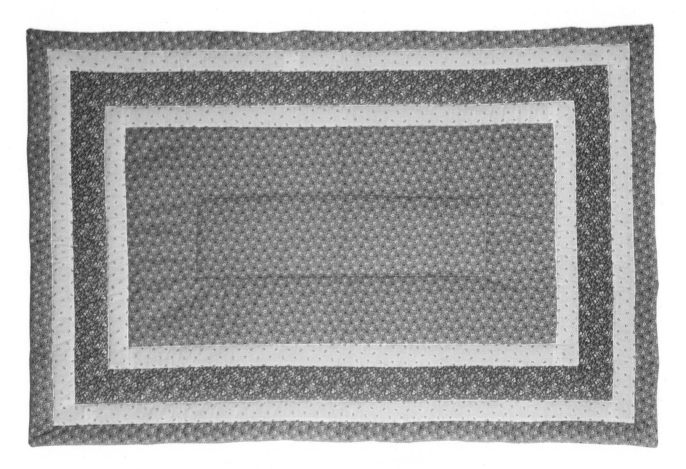

Sweet Dreams Cradle Quilt

A rhapsody of prints, ruffles, and bows turns a simple pieced cradle quilt into a special treasure. The technique for assembling the patchwork top is quick and easy. And you don't need to machine quilt every seamline—bows tacked at block corners secure quilt top, batting, and backing. Design: Gail E. Abeloe.

Gather together . . .

For quilt 30 by 45 inches:

⅜ yard *each* five different pink and burgundy print fabrics, 45 inches wide

¾ yard burgundy gingham fabric

1⅜ yards outing flannel for backing

1 crib-size batting (45 by 60 inches)

15¾ yards pink satin ribbon, ⅛ inch wide

Thread to match backing and ribbon

Yardstick

Piecing the quilt top

Note: Preshrink and press fabrics.

1 On each print fabric, measure and mark three crosswise strips, each 3½ inches wide. Cut strips. Divide strips into three groups, each with five different colors.

2 Arrange strips from one group in a pleasing order. With right sides facing and raw edges aligned, stitch strips together, using ¼-inch seam allowance. Press seams to one side. Repeat with remaining two groups of strips, following same order, to make a total of three pieced rectangles.

3 On each rectangle, measure and mark lines 3½ inches apart crosswise to stitching. Cut on lines—each row of five blocks will be part of a row on quilt top.

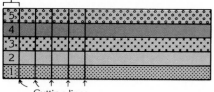

3½ inches

Cutting lines

4 Following layout below, stitch together two five-block rows, using ¼-inch seam allowance, to make first horizontal row; press seams in one direction. Continue piecing rows, alternating direction of pressed seams. (On most rows, you will need to remove a seam, reposition blocks, and restitch to make correct order of blocks.) Stitch horizontal rows together for quilt top; press seams in one direction.

Quilting lines

Patchwork arrangement

5 From gingham, measure, mark, and cut crosswise ruffle strips, each 3 inches wide. Stitch ends together to make one long ruffle strip. With right side out, fold strip in half lengthwise and press.

6 With machine set on longest stitch, make two rows of gathering stitches close to raw edges of ruffle strip. Gather strip to approximately equal perimeter of quilt top. With right sides facing and raw edges aligned, pin gathered strip to quilt top (ruffle points *in*), starting at midpoint of any edge. Allow a little extra ruffle fullness at each corner. Trim end of ruffle so it overlaps beginning by ½ inch. Open out ends of ruffle and, with right sides facing, seam ends; finish pinning ruffle to quilt. Baste ruffle to quilt.

Finishing the quilt

1 Cut batting in half to make two pieces, each 30 by 45 inches. Using quilt top as pattern, cut backing, adding 1 inch to all edges.

2 Lay double layer of batting on floor or table. Over it, place backing, *right side up*, and quilt top, *right*

side down. Pin layers together at edges; trim excess batting.

3 Stitch around edges, leaving most of one short edge open; trim corners. Turn right side out and press lightly. Pin open edge closed.

4 Pin layers together at seamlines marked on diagram under step 4, facing page. Machine quilt (see pages 36—37) along pinned seamlines. Handstitch open edge closed.

5 Cut ribbon into 126 pieces, each 4½ inches long. Fold each piece like a bow, and tack at each block intersection (excluding outside edges), stitching through all layers. See "Beginning the thread" and "Ending the thread," pages 34 and 35, to conceal knots within batting.

Bow

Flying Geese Lap Quilt

You can almost hear a soft flutter of wings when you wrap up in this Flying Geese lap quilt. Like Tree Everlasting, Pineapple, Maple Leaf, and many other traditional quilt designs, the Flying Geese design comes from nature.

Reversing the colors and direction of blocks from row to row gives this particular quilt its flowing, optical quality; very narrow divider strips accentuate changes in pattern. Design: Christine Barnes.

Gather together . . .

For quilt 33 by 49 inches:
1¼ yards *each* navy and burgundy small-print fabric, 45 inches wide
½ yard *each* navy and burgundy lengthwise floral stripe fabric (if you use print without direction, buy only ¼ yard *each* navy and burgundy and cut crosswise strips)
1 yard navy medium-print fabric for backing
¾ yard burgundy medium-print fabric for binding
1½ yards batting, 36 inches wide
Thread, machine and quilting
1 sheet acetate (see page 9)
Craft knife (see page 9)
Metal ruler

Piecing the quilt top

Note: Preshrink and press fabrics.

1 To make paper pattern, carefully draw block design 2 by 4 inches, as shown below. See "Cutting a template," pages 15–16, to make one large and one small triangle template.

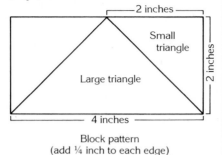

Block pattern
(add ¼ inch to each edge)

2 Read "Cutting pieces," page 16; to save fabric and speed your cutting, place triangles so long edges are on the lengthwise grain and there is no space between pieces. Measure and mark 96 large triangles and 144 small triangles on small burgundy print, and 72 large triangles and 192 small triangles on small navy print. Cut pieces.

3 See "Sewing," pages 16–17, for general piecing instructions. With right sides facing and raw edges aligned, stitch long edge of a small navy triangle to one short edge of a large burgundy triangle, using ¼-inch seam allowance. Fold out small piece and finger-press seam toward edge; stitch another small navy triangle to other edge of burgundy triangle. Repeat for 24 blocks.

Stitch blocks together to form first vertical row; press carefully. Continue making blocks and rows until you have a total of four rows. Using opposite color scheme, make blocks and stitch together to form three vertical rows.

4 From floral stripe fabrics, measure, mark, and cut enough 1-inch-wide strips (piecing, if necessary) to make four navy and four burgundy divider strips, each 49 inches long.

5 With right sides facing and raw edges aligned, stitch alternating navy and burgundy divider strips between rows and to long outside edges. Press quilt top carefully.

Finishing the quilt

1 Measure and mark backing and batting equal to dimensions of quilt top. Cut pieces.

2 See "Assembling the quilt," pages 33–34, to baste three layers together. Read "Outline quilting," page 31, for description of quilting done inside triangles; to handquilt, see pages 34–35.

3 To cut bias for binding from medium-print burgundy fabric, see "Continuous bias casing," pages 38–39; see "Attaching strips," page 39, to finish edges.

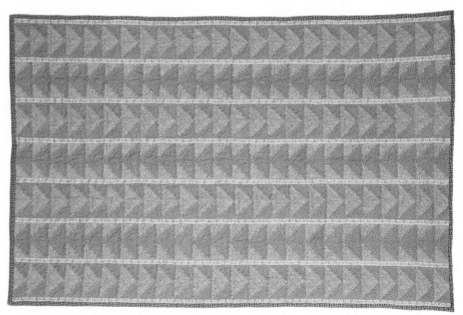

Pastel Pillow Quilt

A pale peach confection of patchwork, this fluffy comforter is a delightful departure from the traditional method of assembling a quilt. The name "pillow quilt" comes from the look you achieve by machine stitching top and backing together and then filling squares individually with layers of batting. A simple gathered skirt finishes the edges.

Gather together . . .

For comforter approximately 40 by 74 inches (without ruffles):

4⅞ yards peach with white print fabric, 45 inches wide
1¼ yards peach with blue print fabric
1¼ yards white with peach print fabric
2¼ yards muslin or print fabric for backing
5¾ yards batting, 54 inches wide
Thread
1 sheet acetate (see page 9)
Craft knife (see page 9)
Metal ruler

Piecing the patchwork top

Note: Preshrink and press fabrics.

1 To make pattern for patchwork square, draw 8-inch square on paper (this includes seam allowance). See "Cutting a template," pages 15–16, to make template from pattern.

(To make a comforter of a different size, measure bed and add about 5 inches to width and 8 inches to length of bed—comforter draws up when filled. Choose a square size that will divide evenly into length and width measurements.)

2 See "Cutting pieces," page 16, for general instructions on cutting patchwork pieces. Before cutting squares from peach with white print, set aside areas for ruffle strips—see "Finishing the Quilt," step 1, for lengths and width. Using template, mark 22 squares on each print except backing fabric. Cut squares.

From batting, measure, mark, and cut 198 squares, each 7 inches.

3 Arrange patchwork squares in rows as shown below to form diagonal pattern. With right sides facing and raw edges aligned, stitch pieces together for first horizontal row, using ¼-inch seam allowance. Press seams in one direction. Continue piecing rows, alternating direction of pressed seams. Stitch rows together. Press; trim edges.

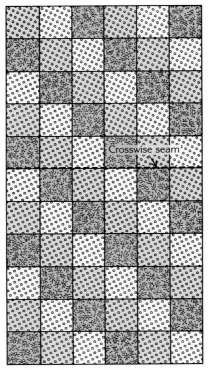

Patchwork arrangement

4 Measure and mark backing equal to size of top. Cut backing.

5 Lay backing, wrong side up, on floor; place patchwork, right side up, over backing. Pin top and backing together along seamline between fifth and sixth crosswise rows. Machine stitch across patchwork top on seamline. Pin and stitch along all lengthwise seams.

6 Starting from either short end, fill each square in row next to stitched crosswise seamline with three layers of batting. Pin and stitch row closed along crosswise seamline. Continue filling and stitching rows to end; turn comforter and work from center to other short end. At head end, bind raw edges with narrow strip of one of top print fabrics.

Finishing the quilt

1 On peach with white print, measure and mark two ruffle strips 12½ inches by 4¼ yards, and one ruffle strip 12½ inches by 2¼ yards. Cut strips.

2 On ends of each ruffle strip, turn under raw edges twice; press and stitch. On one lengthwise edge of each strip, turn under 1 inch twice; press and stitch hem.

3 Gather long strips to match sides of comforter, and short strip to fit end. With right sides facing, pin and stitch ruffles to comforter.

Baskets Wall Hanging

Bright baskets of flowers bloom against a periwinkle background on this graphic quilted hanging. The gemlike colors and geometric pieces typify the popular Amish basket designs.

Like traditional basket quilts, this contemporary interpretation combines iridescent colors with black to create a radiant pieced top. Outline quilting sets off baskets; simple wreaths decorate plain blocks. Design: Sara Halpern Robb.

Gather together . . .

For one basket hanging, 41 inches square:
- 1 yard periwinkle blue fabric
- 1 yard black fabric
- ¾ yard magenta fabric
- ¼ yard *each* dark red, purple, blue green, moss green, pumpkin, and red orange fabrics
- 1¼ yards print fabric, 45 inches wide, for backing
- 1¼ yards batting, at least 45 inches wide
- Thread, black sewing and quilting
- 2 sheets acetate (see page 9)
- Craft knife (see page 9)
- Metal ruler
- Graph paper

Piecing the patchwork

Note: Preshrink and press fabrics.

1 On graph paper, carefully enlarge basket block design shown at right. On patterns, *add ¼-inch seam allowance to all edges* of large triangle, small triangle, and rectangle. (In hanging shown in photo, each basket is composed of five pieces—four small triangles and one square. To simplify cutting and piecing, our pattern combines square and two lower triangles into one large triangle.)

To make patterns for periwinkle background blocks, edge triangles, and corner triangles, draw a 7-inch square on graph paper, and divide as shown above, next column. *Add ¼-inch seam allowance to all edges.*

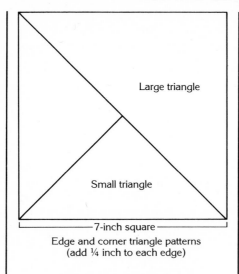

Edge and corner triangle patterns
(add ¼ inch to each edge)

See "Cutting a template," pages 15–16, to cut templates from patterns. Label templates for background triangles and basket block triangles so you don't confuse them.

2 Following general instructions under "Cutting pieces," page 16, cut pieces from fabrics specified.

From black fabric, using basket block templates, cut 16 large triangles, 128 small triangles, and 32 rectangles. Measure, mark, and cut four binding strips 3 by 45 inches.

From magenta fabric, using basket block templates, cut two large triangles and 34 small triangles. Measure, mark, and cut 32 inner border strips 1¼ by 6½ inches, 32 inner border strips 1¼ by 7½ inches, and four outer border strips 1¼ by 45 inches.

From periwinkle fabric using basket block templates, cut two large triangles and 16 small triangles. From same fabric, using background templates, cut 12 edge triangles, four corner triangles, and nine squares.

Cut additional basket block triangles as follows: from dark red, two large and 12 small; from moss green, five large and 14 small; from blue green, two large and eight small; from purple, two large and eight small; from pumpkin, one large and 28 small; from red orange, eight small.

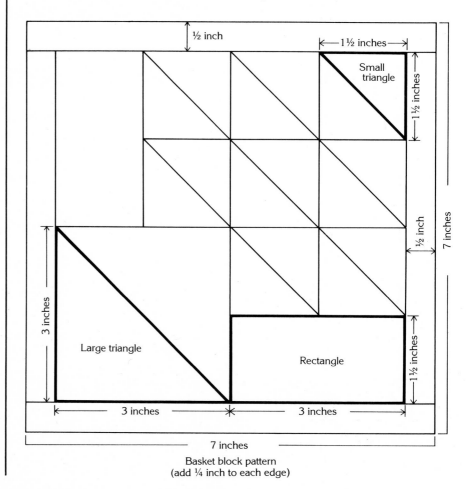

Basket block pattern
(add ¼ inch to each edge)

3 Follow color combinations listed below to compose basket blocks:

Two baskets each: moss green basket with two blue green and four magenta flowers; moss green basket with four pumpkin and two magenta flowers; periwinkle basket with four red orange and two magenta flowers; blue green basket with four magenta and two periwinkle flowers; purple basket with four pumpkin and two moss green flowers; magenta basket with four dark red and two pumpkin flowers.

One basket each: dark red basket with four purple and two magenta flowers; dark red basket with four pumpkin and two periwinkle flowers; pumpkin basket with four magenta and two periwinkle flowers; moss green basket with four periwinkle and two pumpkin flowers.

4 For easy piecing of your first basket block (moss green basket with blue green and magenta flowers), think of the square as divided into quarters. You construct each quarter, then sew quarters together.

Begin with lower left quarter. With right sides facing and raw edges aligned, stitch large black and moss green triangles together on long edges, using ¼-inch seam allowance. Press seam, and all seams that follow, to one side.

Next, assemble upper left quarter. Stitch small black and magenta triangles together; repeat with black and moss green. Sew resulting two small squares together to form rectangle; stitch to black rectangle.

Repeat same sequence to assemble lower right quarter.

To construct upper right quarter, stitch pairs of triangles together to make four small squares. Stitch two squares together to make rectangle; repeat with remaining two squares. Stitch rectangles together.

5 Stitch lower quarters together, then join upper quarters. To complete block, stitch large rectangles together.

Repeat steps to make a total of 16 baskets in color combinations listed above, at left.

6 To attach magenta borders to basket blocks, stitch 1¼ by 6½-inch strips to side edges of squares; press seams toward outside edges. Stitch 1¼ by 7½-inch strips to top and bottom edges; press seams toward outside edges.

7 Using photo as a guide, set quilt top, placing baskets on point to form diamonds. It's easiest to stitch basket blocks and periwinkle background pieces together into diagonal rows, then stitch rows together.

8 To attach outer magenta borders, sew long strips to side edges of quilt top; trim excess off ends and press seams toward outside edges. Sew remaining strips to quilt top and bottom; trim ends and press.

9 Carefully press pieced top. On graph paper, enlarge wreath quilting pattern below. See "Transferring patterns," pages 32–33, to transfer design to centers of plain blocks. Quilting pattern in edge and corner triangles consists of diagonal rows of triangles the size of *finished* basket flowers.

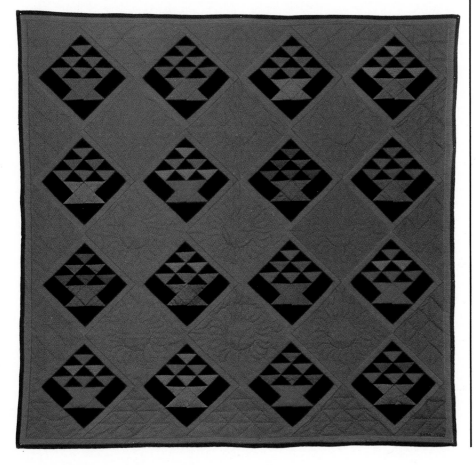

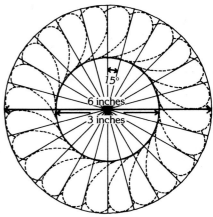

Wreath quilting pattern

Making the hanging

1 Cut backing and batting 1 inch larger on each edge than pieced top. See "Basting the quilt," page 33, to stitch three layers together.

2 With black quilting thread, hand-quilt (see pages 34–35) periwinkle background blocks and triangles.

3 See "Attaching strips," page 39, to finish edges with black binding strips.

Houses Wall Hanging

"Can you come out and play?" Offering hours of imaginary play with make-believe friends, a dozen identical houses line the streets of this cheery little quilt. Our pieced and appliquéd house block is a classic design often seen on both antique and new quilts; if you prefer, reproduce your own home in fabric for a very personal wall hanging. Design: Diana Leone.

Gather together . . .

For hanging 24½ by 32 inches:
¾ yard green print fabric for dividers, squares, paths, borders, and binding
⅜ yard dark blue print for sky
¼ yard brown stripe fabric for roofs
¼ yard light green print fabric for sides of houses
¼ yard light green and orange print fabric for fronts of houses
¼ yard floral print fabric for gardens, squares, borders, and binding
⅛ yard burgundy print fabric for chimneys
⅛ yard yellow dotted fabric for doors
⅛ yard light blue print fabric for windows
1 yard white or print fabric for backing
1 yard batting, at least 36 inches wide
Thread, sewing and quilting
1 sheet acetate (see page 9)
Craft knife (see page 9)
Metal ruler

Piecing the blocks

Note: Preshrink and press fabrics.

1 To make individual pattern pieces, trace each shape from full-size pattern, shown on facing page, onto paper. *To each edge, add ¼-inch seam allowance.* See "Cutting a template," pages 15–16, to cut templates from these patterns.

2 Read "Cutting pieces," page 16, for general cutting hints. Before cutting pieces from green or floral prints, set aside areas for divider strips, border strips, and binding strips—see "Adding dividers and borders," step 1, and "Finishing the hanging," step 3, for strip lengths and widths.

For 12 blocks, measure and mark the following pieces on fabrics specified: templates A, B, C, D, E, F, G—from dark blue print, 12 pieces each; templates H, I—from burgundy print, 12 pieces each; templates J, K, L—from light green and orange print, 12 pieces each; template M—from yellow dot, 12 pieces; template N—from brown stripe, 12 pieces; templates O, P, Q—from light green print, 12 pieces each; template R—from light blue print, 12 pieces; template S (rectangle)—from floral print, 12 pieces; and template T—from green print, 12 pieces. Cut pieces.

3 Read "Sewing," pages 16–17, for instructions and tips on hand and machine piecing. Refer to pattern as you piece blocks.

With right sides facing and raw edges aligned, stitch pieces together to make rows, using ¼-inch seam allowance. (In first and third rows, stitch small pieces together first.) Press seams in one direction, away from bulk.

On fourth row, appliqué (see pages 24–25) each path shape to each ground piece. Stitch rows together to form blocks. Press blocks and trim to 6-inch squares.

Adding dividers and borders

1 On green print fabric, measure and mark 17 divider strips 2 by 6½

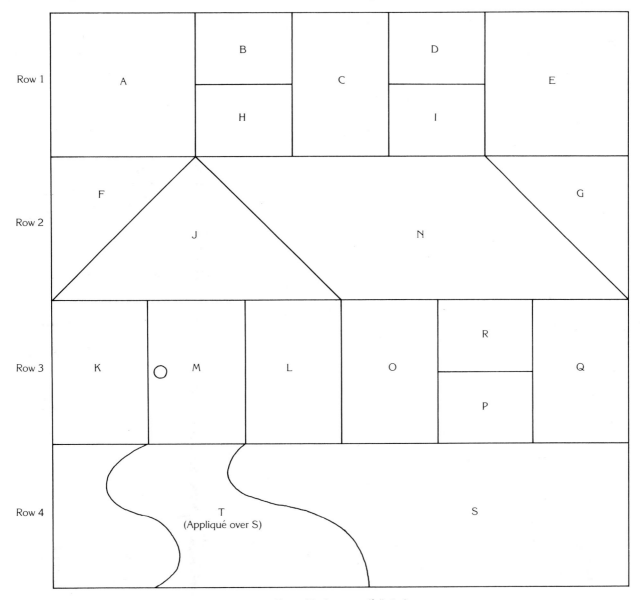

Row 1: A, B, C, D, E, H, I

Row 2: F, J, N, G

Row 3: K, M, L, O, R, Q, P

Row 4: T (Appliqué over S), S

House block pattern (full size)
(add ¼ inch to each edge)

inches, four side border strips 2 by 14 inches, one top border strip 2 by 21½ inches, and two bottom corner squares 2 by 2 inches. Cut pieces.

On floral print, measure and mark one bottom border strip 2 by 21½ inches, and 12 squares 2 by 2 inches. Cut pieces.

2 With right sides facing and raw edges aligned, stitch vertical divider strips to house blocks to form each row; press seams toward dividers.

To piece horizontal dividers, stitch two floral squares between three divider strips as shown above, next column. Stitch these dividers between rows, matching seamlines.

Divider strip

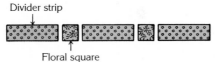

Floral square

3 To piece each side border, stitch a floral square between two 14-inch green border strips; add another floral square to end of second green strip. Attach side borders at side edges of pieced top.

For top border, stitch floral squares to both ends of 21½-inch green border strip. To make bottom border, stitch green print squares to both ends of 21½-inch floral border strip. Attach borders to top and bottom edges. Press top.

Finishing the hanging

1 Cut backing and batting slightly larger than pieced top. See "Basting the quilt," page 33, to stitch three layers together.

2 Using quilting thread, outline quilt (see pages 31 and 34–35) main house shapes and dividers.

3 For top and bottom edges, measure and mark two binding strips 3 by 26½ inches on green print; for side edges, measure and mark two binding strips 3 by 34 inches on floral print. Cut strips. See "Attaching strips," page 39, to finish edges.

Off-center Log Cabin

Lopsided blocks give a kaleidoscopic effect to this innovative off-center log cabin hanging. Logs of two different widths move the center square from the middle; the off-center look is accentuated by the use of light and dark solids and prints.

Examine this hanging and you'll see that the corner blocks are identical, as are the four center blocks, but pairs of side blocks are put together to be mirror images of each other. Design: Ann A. Rhode.

Gather together . . .

For quilt hanging 47 inches square:
- ⅜ yard melon fabric
- ¼ yard *each* purple and brown fabrics
- ¼ yard *each* coral, beige, salmon, and pale peach fabrics
- ¼ yard *each* three dark print fabrics
- ⅜ yard dark print fabric
- ¼ yard *each* four light print fabrics
- ⅛ yard burgundy print fabric for borders
- 3 yards dark print fabric for backing
- ⅝ yard burgundy fabric for binding
- 1½ yards batting, 54 inches wide
- Thread, quilting and sewing

Assembling the blocks

Note: Preshrink and press fabrics.

1 Before cutting log strips from melon, brown, and dark print border fabrics, set aside areas for border strips — see "Assembling the quilt," step 2, for lengths and widths.

To cut fabric into strips, see "Log Cabin quilt construction," page 19, second paragraph. Cut 2-inch-wide strips from solid fabrics, and 1¼-inch-wide strips from print fabrics (except backing fabric). From off-white fabric, cut sixteen 2-inch squares.

2 Refer to diagram and photo as you assemble 16 blocks. Construct blocks according to railroading method described in "A quilted log cabin quilt," page 20.

Start with four center blocks (A). Using four light prints and three light solids, stitch four identical blocks. Begin by stitching light print strip to center square; then spiral out. (In setting quilt, blocks will be rotated.)

3 Next, stitch four identical corner blocks (B), using four dark prints and three dark solids; begin by stitching dark print strip to center square.

4 Blocks C and D sit side by side in pairs in quilt top and are mirror images of each other. To begin each block, stitch dark print strip to center square. When you line up resulting pieces along second dark print strip, position pieces so four of attached dark print strips are *on left of center squares,* and four are *on right*. (To avoid confusion, construct C blocks, then construct D blocks.)

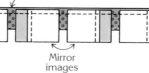

Second dark print strip

Mirror images

If you study diagram and photo, you'll see that prints are always used in pairs and follow same order as print logs in corner blocks.

Solid strips are not in pairs. Stitch solids as follows: *first* solid strip is same color as third dark solid (brown) in B blocks; *second* solid strip is same color as first light solid (coral) in A; *third* solid strip is same color as second dark solid (purple) in B; *fourth* solid strip is same color as second light solid (beige) in A; *fifth* solid strip is same color as first dark solid (melon) in B; *sixth* solid strip is fourth light solid (pale peach), not used before. Press blocks; measure and trim so all are same size.

Assembling the quilt

1 Arrange 16 blocks as shown. With right sides facing and raw edges aligned, stitch blocks together into rows, using ¼-inch seam allowance. Stitch rows together for quilt top.

2 On remaining melon fabric, measure and mark four inner border

Quilt top

strips 1½ by 40 inches; on remaining brown fabric, measure and mark four strips 1 by 40 inches. On burgundy print fabric, measure and mark four outer border strips 6 by 50 inches. Cut strips.

3 See "Borders," page 30, to stitch border strips together, attach them to quilt edges, and miter corners.

4 See "Quilting designs," pages 31–32, for information on quilting patterns. (Log cabin shown here has lines of quilting radiating from central area, outline quilting around dark solid strips, and large modified diamond quilting design in borders.)

To transfer designs to quilt top, see "Transferring patterns," pages 32–33.

5 Measure, mark, and cut batting equal to dimensions of quilt top. Cut backing into two equal lengths, each 1½ yards. With right sides facing, sew pieces together along selvage edges, using ⅝-*inch seam allowance.* Cut off selvages and press seam open. Assemble quilt top, batting, and backing according to instructions in "Assembling the quilt," pages 33–34. To handquilt, see pages 34–35.

6 On burgundy fabric, measure and mark four binding strips 4½ by 52 inches. Cut strips. See "Attaching strips," page 39, to finish edges.

Child's String Vest

There's a rainbow out every time your child wears this string-quilted vest in bright crayon hues. Working on the batting and lining together, you attach strips and do the quilting all in one step. Printed bias tape, the folds pressed out, conceals side and shoulder seam allowances; the same tape stitched to armhole and outside edges makes the vest reversible. Trim the front with grosgrain ribbon; on the back, appliqué a delicate crocheted heart or a snippet of special lace. Design: Heidi Weiss.

Gather together . . .

Note: Yardage requirements are for child's size 6.

½ yard print fabric for lining
¼ yard *each* seven bright print fabrics for strips
½ yard bonded batting
2 packages extra-wide, double-fold bias tape
　Simple vest pattern (no darts)
　Thread to match lining
½ yard grosgrain ribbon, 1 inch wide
　Crocheted heart or piece of lace (optional)
　Indelible marking pen (see page 9)
　Marking pencil (see page 9)
　Metal ruler

Stitching the strips

Note: Preshrink and press fabrics.

1 On any print except lining fabric, measure and mark, with pencil, a piece 3½ by 4 inches for center back. Cut piece.

To make cutting strips easier, fold each fabric except lining fabric lengthwise into quarters. Measure and mark, with pencil, crosswise strips varying in width from 1 to 1¾ inches. Cut strips. You can also use lengths of bias tape, with folds pressed out, as strips.

2 Using vest pattern, cut one back and two front pieces *each* from lining fabric and batting. Pin each batting piece to wrong side of matching lining piece.

3 Using ruler and indelible marking pen, measure and mark two vertical lines on back batting piece 1¾ inches from center back line.

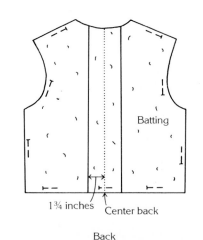

1¾ inches　　Center back

Back

On each front batting piece, measure and mark a horizontal line starting at underarm and a vertical line in center of each lower front half. (These lines will guide you as you attach strips and quilt.)

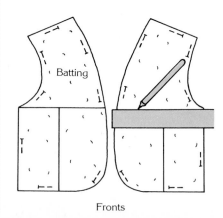

Fronts

4 Arrange strips on batting pieces, using lines as guides. Carefully set strips aside in order.

5 Begin working on vest back. With batting face up, place back center piece, right side up, between two vertical guidelines and pin.

6 With right sides facing, pin first strip to lower edge of center piece. Using ¼-inch seam allowance, stitch through all thicknesses between vertical guidelines. (Make sure bobbin thread matches lining.)

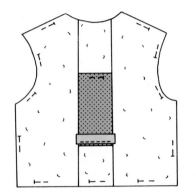

Back

Fold strip right side up and finger-press seam; trim excess from ends of strip. Stitch second strip to first in same manner. Continue working to bottom edge; then work from center piece to neck edge.

7 Attach vertical strips to both sides of center back piece in same way. Trim ends of strips even with outside edges of back.

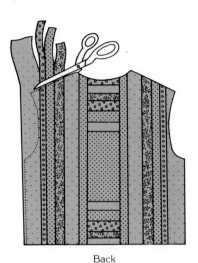

Back

8 To stitch each vest front, place first strip, right side up, over vertical guideline and pin. Stitch all strips from center strip to one edge, then turn vest and work to other edge.

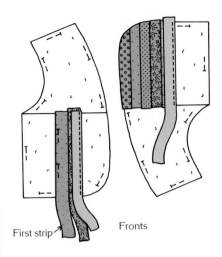

First strip   Fronts

9 Attach first horizontal strip so it covers ends of vertical strips. Continue working to shoulder edge.

10 Pin and topstitch rainbow ribbon to vest fronts as shown.

Assembling the vest

1 *With wrong sides facing*, pin and stitch shoulder seams and side seams together, using ⅝-inch seam allowance. Press seams open.

2 To cover shoulder and side seam allowances, press open a piece of bias tape 28 inches long. With right side of vest facing up, center a length of bias strip over each seamline and pin. Turn edges of strip under seam allowances to encase raw edges. Pin and stitch close to edges through all thicknesses. Trim ends of strip even with vest edges.

3 To make ties, cut two 10-inch lengths of folded bias tape, and stitch close to each open folded edge of tape. Baste each tie to vest front just below ribbon trim.

4 Pin and stitch bias tape to raw edges of vest. Make sure ends of strips, batting, and lining get caught in stitching.

5 If you wish, appliqué crocheted heart or lace to center back.

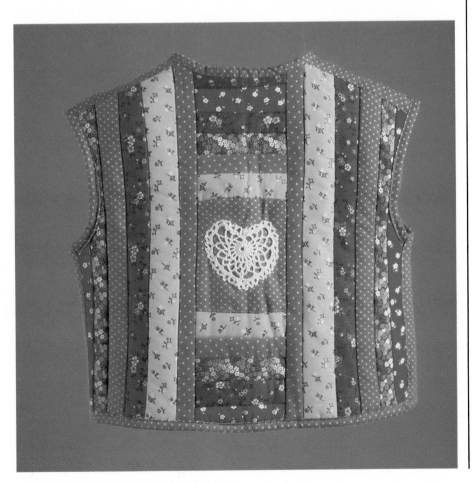

String Quilted Jacket

Inspired by the wide range of beautiful desert hues, this sophisticated string jacket is pieced and quilted at the same time. The quilting occurs as you stitch strips together on the batting and lining.

The subtle piecing and arrangement of colored strips of varying lengths and widths create an abstract landscape across the jacket. Prairie points, small folded squares tucked into seams, accent the jacket's vertical lines. Design: Sonya Lee Barrington.

Gather together . . .

For one jacket:
Note: Yardage requirements are for size 12.

¼ yard *each* teal, forest green, moss green, dark brown, rust, salmon, mushroom, and fuchsia fabrics, 45 inches wide

3 yards muslin, 45 inches wide

1½ yards lightweight batting, 45 inches wide

Simple jacket pattern (no darts)

Thread to match muslin

Metal ruler

Indelible marking pen (see page 9)

Cutting the strips

Note: Preshrink and press fabrics.

1 To make cutting strips easier, fold each colored fabric lengthwise into quarters. On each piece, mark crosswise strips in three widths: 1, 1½, and 2 inches. Cut strips.

2 See "Separate bias strips," page 38, to cut and seam 1¼-inch-wide muslin bias strips to make 3½ yards. Set strip aside.

3 Lay muslin, right side down, on floor or table; place batting over muslin. Position pattern pieces over batting so lengths of back, fronts, and sleeves are on crosswise grain. Adding approximately 3 inches to all edges (pieces draw up a little when stitched), cut pieces. Set pattern pieces aside. Pin batting and backing together at edges.

Measure, mark, and cut remaining muslin into strips of three different widths as you did colored fabrics. From leftover muslin, cut 2-inch squares for prairie points (jacket shown has 46). Form points as shown below, pressing each fold as you go. Set points aside.

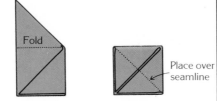

4 Using ruler and indelible marking pen, mark vertical center line on each piece of batting. These lines will guide you as you attach strips.

Stitching the strips

1 Arrange strips and prairie points on batting to make a design you like. (See photo for ideas on color and size arrangement of strips.) Carefully set strips aside in order.

To top of each colored strip, stitch a muslin strip of matching width to make a pieced strip slightly longer than pattern piece. Trim excess muslin and save remnants—sometimes you'll need only a short strip. Finger-press seams down.

2 Begin working on jacket back. Place center strip, right side up, over center line on batting. With right sides facing, pin second strip to right-hand edge of center strip. Using ¼-inch seam allowance, stitch along edge through all thicknesses. Fold strip right side up, and finger-press seam. In same manner, stitch third strip to left-hand edge of center strip.

Continue stitching strips, alternating sides and inserting prairie points in seams as desired, until jacket back is covered. Stitch strips to jacket front and sleeves in same manner.

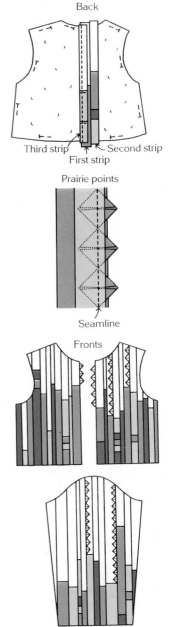

Back

Third strip — Second strip

First strip

Prairie points

Seamline

Fronts

Sleeve

Finishing the jacket

1 Reposition patterns on jacket pieces and recut to exact sizes. Assemble jacket according to pattern instructions.

2 With right sides facing and raw edges aligned, pin muslin bias binding, cutting off lengths as needed, to edges of neck, fronts, bottom, and cuffs. To pivot at corners, clip *almost* ½ inch into bias binding. Stitch binding to edges, using ½-inch seam allowance. Clip neck curves. Fold binding to inside, turn under ¼ inch, and handstitch to muslin lining. At corners, fold in excess.

Trapunto Purse

Step out with this elegant evening bag and you'll be carrying an example of the ultimate in quilting techniques—trapunto. Intricate blooms, outline stitched and then stuffed from the back, decorate the inner envelope and one that slips over it. Back pockets on each make this purse-within-a-purse as useful as it is pretty. Design: Marjorie Murphy.

Gather together . . .

For one purse 8 by 7 inches:
⅜ yard pale peach fabric, 45 inches wide
⅜ yard deep peach fabric
⅜ yard batting
    Thread, sewing and quilting, to match fabrics
    Needles, quilting and tapestry
    4-ply white acrylic yarn for trapunto

Stitching the purse

Note: Preshrink and press fabrics.

1 Trace patterns and quilting designs for outer (larger) and inner (smaller) purses and pockets. See "Enlarging designs," steps 2–6, page 22, to enlarge tracings to full-size patterns in dimensions given.

2 Fold each piece of fabric in half lengthwise. Adding 1 inch to all edges, cut two outer purse pieces from pale peach fabric, and two inner pieces from deep peach fabric (pockets are cut as part of purse pieces). Cut one batting piece the same size as outer purse and one piece the same size as inner purse.

3 Using one of the methods described in "Transferring patterns," pages 32–33, transfer quilting designs, cutting lines, and seamlines to one outer and one inner purse piece.

4 Place unmarked outer piece, wrong side up, on table. Over it, lay matching batting piece and marked outer piece, right side up. Baste layers together. Repeat for inner purse pieces.

5 Handquilt (see pages 34–35) floral designs on both pieces, then quilt diamond pattern just to seamlines.

6 To do trapunto, see "Stuffing designs" under "Corded quilting," page 36. Insert needle at tip of each petal, and come out at base.

7 Reposition patterns on quilted pieces and recut along cutting lines. Cut pockets apart from main purse sections.

On remaining pale peach fabric, measure and mark one binding strip 1½ by 28 inches, and one shoulder strap 1 by 45 inches. On deep peach fabric, measure and mark one binding strip 1½ by 28 inches. Cut strips. Cut holes for strap on outer purse as shown, and finish edges by hand with buttonhole stitch (see page 24).

Assembling the purse

1 With right side out, fold pale peach binding strip in half lengthwise, and press fold. Cut a length of strip equal to long edge of pale peach pocket. With right sides facing and raw edges aligned, machine stitch strip to long edge, using ¼-inch seam allowance. Fold strip to back and handstitch to conceal machine stitching. Repeat with deep peach strip and pocket.

2 Place pale peach pocket on unstuffed half of outer purse so raw edges are aligned and bound edge is on placement line. Baste pocket to purse around three raw edges.

Trapunto purse patterns
(¼-inch seam allowance included)

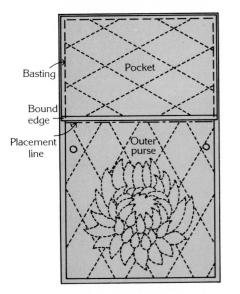

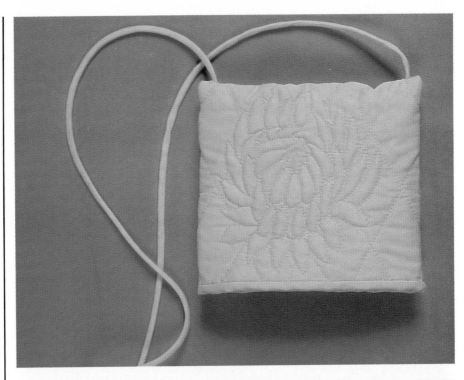

Fold purse so right sides are facing and raw edges aligned (pocket will be inside). Pin and stitch sides together; turn right side out and bind open edge.

3 On inner purse, position pocket on stuffed half so long unbound edge is on placement line and pocket almost covers flower. Stitch pocket to purse on placement line. Fold pocket out, press lightly, and baste to purse at side edges. Fold and stitch inner purse together in same manner as for outer purse; bind open edge.

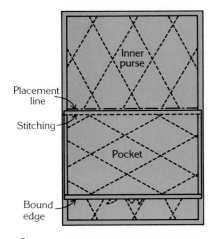

4 With right sides facing, fold strap in half lengthwise and stitch. Turn right side out (a loop turner, available at fabric stores, is helpful).

5 Lay purses, trapunto sides up, so bound open edges touch. String ends of strap through holes and attach at inner purse side seams.

Roman Stripe Tied Quilt

Like abstract boats sailing on a glassy gray sea, colorful pieced triangles combine with plain ones to make the blocks in this stunning tied quilt. Inspired by Amish Roman Stripe quilts, this contemporary version has one major difference: streaks of color run horizontally rather than diagonally across the quilt blocks. Design: Beth Ann Sjoblom Stoebner.

Gather together . . .

For quilt approximately 85 by 90 inches:

- 3 yards pearl gray fabric, 45 inches wide
- 1¾ yards *each* lavender, wine, and purple fabrics for stripes and borders, 45 inches wide
- ½ yard *each* blue, raspberry, and teal fabrics for stripes, 45 inches wide
- 8¼ yards black fabric for backing
- 11¼ yards batting, 54 inches wide
- Thread, black
- Embroidery floss, 6 skeins pearl gray
- 1 sheet acetate (see page 9)
- Craft knife (see page 9)
- Metal ruler
- Plastic ruler, 2 inches wide

Piecing the quilt top

Note: Preshrink and press fabrics.

1 Using width of plastic ruler as guide, mark eight crosswise strips, each 2 inches wide, on each fabric except gray and black. Cut strips and divide into eight groups, each with six different colored strips.

2 Arrange strips from one group in order shown in photo, or arrange as desired. With right sides facing and raw edges aligned, stitch strips together, using ¼-inch seam allowance. Press seams in one direction. Repeat with other groups of strips to make a total of eight rectangles, each 9½ inches wide.

3 Trim end of one rectangle so it's perpendicular to long edges. Starting at trimmed end, measure and mark four lines 9½ inches apart crosswise

to stitching. Cut on lines to make four squares, each 9½ inches. Repeat on other rectangles. Fold each square in half diagonally and press; cut along fold to make 64 striped triangles.

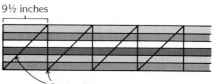

9½ inches

Cutting lines

4 On gray fabric, measure and mark 32 squares, each 9½ inches. Cut pieces to make 64 triangles.

5 With right sides facing and long raw edges aligned, stitch gray triangles and striped triangles together for 64 blocks. Press seams toward gray triangles.

Resulting blocks will not be exactly square. To make them square, use metal ruler and craft knife to cut 9-inch-square acetate template (see pages 15–16). Placing diagonally opposite corners of template on diagonal seamline of each block, mark around template; trim edges.

6 Starting with block that has bottom stripe of purple and alternating with squares with bottom stripe of lavender, stitch eight squares together for first horizontal row. Press seams in one direction. Repeat for seven more rows, alternating color of first block in each row. Change direction of pressed seams from row to row.

Stitch rows together to form quilt top, being careful to make points of triangles meet at corners. Press seams in one direction.

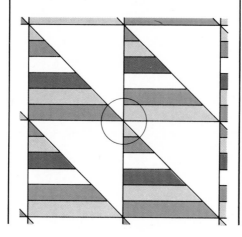

Adding borders

1 On remaining gray fabric, measure and mark four crosswise strips 4½ inches wide and four strips 6½ inches wide. On each of wine, purple, and lavender fabrics, measure and mark eight strips 3½ inches wide. Cut strips. Stitch together ends of 4½-inch-wide gray strips to make a long strip; repeat with 6½-inch-wide gray strips. Also seam ends of wine, purple, and lavender strips to form three long strips of each color.

Cut off proper lengths of border strips as you need them and attach to quilt top. Starting at top and bottom edges, attach 6½-inch-wide gray strips to quilt top, using ¼-inch seam allowance. Press seams, and all seams that follow, toward borders. Attach 4½-inch-wide gray strips to side edges.

Add wine, purple, and lavender borders in same manner. Press top carefully. Quilt top should measure approximately 83 by 88 inches.

Finishing the quilt

1 For backing, cut black fabric into three equal lengths. With right sides facing and selvage edges aligned, stitch lengths together, using ½-inch seam allowance. Cut off selvages and press seams open. Measure, mark, and trim backing to 95 by 100 inches.

2 Cut batting into four lengths, each 100 inches. Whipstitch two pieces together along long edges; repeat with other two pieces. Stack pieces for double layer of batting.

3 Lay backing, wrong side up, on floor. Place double layer of batting over backing and trim excess batting to edges of backing. Center quilt top, right side up, on batting and backing; pin layers together at every block.

4 Bring backing and batting forward to quilt top, turning under ¼-inch seam allowance to form 3-inch-deep black border. Pin through all thicknesses. To miter corners, bring each corner point forward so it overlaps corner point of quilt top as shown at right. Then fold straight edges forward to form miter.

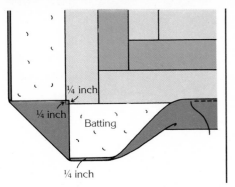

Stitch backing to quilt top through all thicknesses close to inside folded edge. Also stitch ½ inch from outside edge.

5 Using six strands of embroidery floss, tie quilt (see page 37) at corners of blocks, at midpoints of diagonal seams, and at evenly spaced intervals within borders as shown at right. Trim ties to desired length. Remove pins.

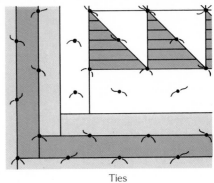

Ties

Double Irish Chain Quilt

One of the best known and loved patchwork patterns, the Double Irish Chain forms dramatic diagonal bands that float on a solid background. Though the design looks intricate, it actually consists of only two alternating blocks, one five-patch and one plain block with small squares appliquéd at each corner.

Gather together . . .

For quilt approximately 90 by 104 inches:

5¾ yards white fabric, 45 inches wide

3½ yards navy fabric

1½ yards pin-dot navy fabric

8¼ yards white or muslin fabric

  6 yards batting, at least 45 inches wide

    Thread, white sewing and quilting

  1 sheet acetate (see page 9)

    Craft knife (see page 9)

    Metal ruler

    Yardstick

    Graph paper

Piecing the quilt top

Note: Preshrink and press fabrics.

1 Quilt top, excluding borders, is made up of alternating patchwork and white blocks, and is 10 blocks wide and 12 blocks long.

To make pattern for large square, draw square 7⅜ inches (this includes seam allowance) on graph paper. See "Cutting a template," pages 15–16, to make large template from pattern. You needn't cut a template for small squares; since there are so many, it's faster to measure and mark them with a yardstick.

2 Before cutting squares from navy and white fabrics, set aside areas for border strips—see steps 6 and 7, opposite, for border lengths and widths.

Following instructions under "Cutting pieces," page 16, measure and mark pieces as follows: 960 small squares on navy fabric, 540 small squares on pin-dot fabric, and 240 small squares and 60 large squares on white fabric. Cut pieces.

3 Follow arrangement shown on facing page to assemble five-patch block. Stitch individual squares into rows by hand or machine (see "Sewing," pages 16–17); then stitch rows together to complete blocks. Each finished block should measure 7⅜ inches square.

4 For plain white block with navy corners, turn under ¼ inch on two edges of four small navy squares, and press. With right sides up and raw edges aligned, pin pieces in corners of large white square. Use hidden hemming stitch (see page 24) to sew pressed edges to block; baste raw edges together within seam allowances. Repeat for a total of 60 white blocks.

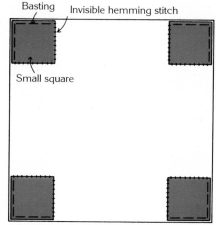

White block

5 Starting with patchwork block and alternating patchwork with white blocks, stitch 10 blocks together for first horizontal row. Begin second row with white block, third with patchwork block. Continue stitching blocks into rows in this manner for a total of 12 rows; stitch rows together to form quilt top. Top should measure 69¼ by 83 inches.

6 On remaining navy fabric, measure and mark four 3-inch-wide inner border strips: two 74¼ inches long, plus several inches; and two 88 inches long, plus several inches. Cut strips. See "Borders," page 30, to attach strips to patchwork top and to miter corners.

7 On remaining white fabric, measure and mark four 8-inch-wide strips: two 89¾ inches long, plus several inches; and two 103½ inches long, plus several inches. Cut strips. Attach to edges of navy borders, mitering corners. Press quilt top carefully.

Finishing the quilt

1 See "Quilting designs," pages 31–32, for information on types of quilting patterns. Outline quilt patchwork pieces on two of four edges; quilt simple flower motif in each white block. Some possibilities for border quilting designs are feathers, diamonds, and cables.

To mark designs on quilt top, see "Transferring patterns," pages 32–33.

2 For backing, cut fabric into three equal lengths. With right sides facing and selvage edges aligned, stitch lengths together, using ½-inch seam allowance. Cut off selvages and press seams open.

3 To put together quilt top, batting, and backing, see "Assembling the quilt," pages 33–34. See "Handquilting," pages 34–35, for quilting instructions.

4 From remaining white fabric, cut approximately 11 yards of 3½-inch-wide bias binding following instructions for "Continuous bias casing," pages 38–39. See "Attaching strips," page 39, to finish edges.

Five-patch block

Projects **69**

A Gallery of Quilts

Why the endless fascination with quilts? Once an absolute necessity, they are no longer *needed*, exactly. Instead, they are *wanted*, loved, cherished — for their magnificent designs, for their awe-inspiring artistry, and for the tales their stitches tell.

Today, America is experiencing an explosive revival in quilting. For some quiltmakers and collectors, the traditional motifs and methods are the ones to be treasured; for others, this great resource of American folk art is a departure point for original techniques and designs.

You may be thinking about making your first quilt, or you may have family heirlooms you'd like to display. Either way, this collection of antique and contemporary quilting will provide inspiration.

On these two pages we show you Amish, a distinctive quilting tradition that excites collectors and provides a rich source of inspiration for contemporary quiltmakers. Study these quilts and the ones on the following 16 pages, and you'll gain a greater sense of appreciation for this art form. Then take tradition into *your* hands and stitch your own bit of quilt history.

Elaborate quilting of Diamond in Square, a favorite Amish pattern, adds subtle texture to jewel-like hues and simplicity of design. Collection of Edward Brown.

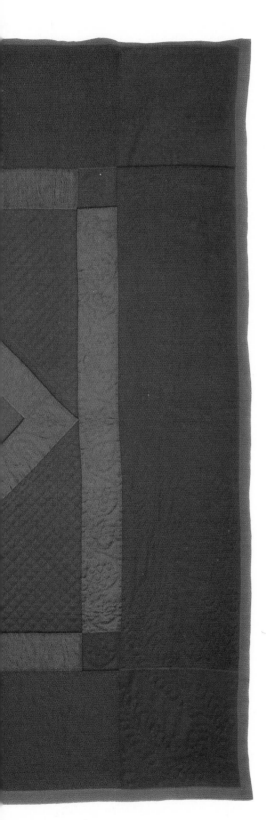

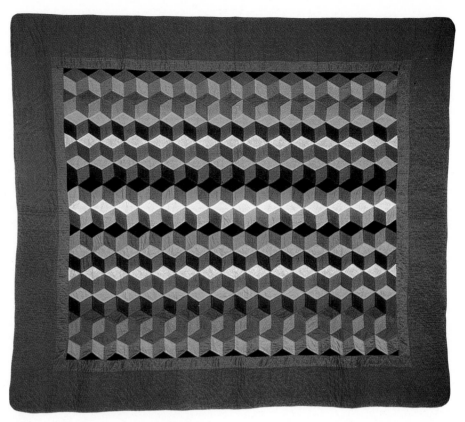

Like an optical illusion, Baby Blocks float on Amish quilt, circa 1930. Collection of Mr. and Mrs. Nicholas R. Cox.

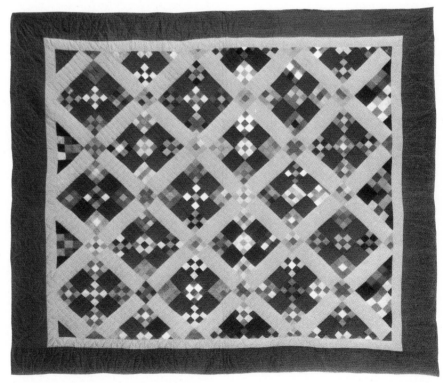

Crisscrossing divides blocks of Indiana Amish Double Nine-Patch. Collection of Once Upon A Quilt.

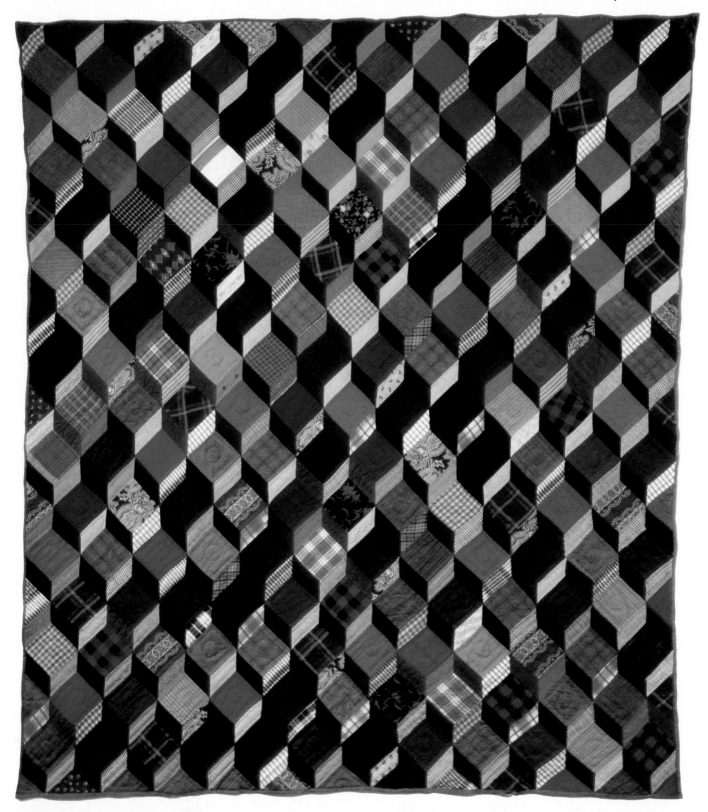

Elongated diamonds form Tumbling Blocks variation on one side of 19th century reversible quilt. Design on wool backing (not shown) is square block within borders. Collection of Once Upon A Quilt.

Potpourri of pieced quilts — movement and color unite for dramatic designs

Plaid effect of Nine-Patch quilt, contained in border of Flying Geese, is achieved by selective use of color. Design: Sara Halpern Robb.

Random-size velvet and silk pieces make up Victorian crazy quilt; monograms and embroidery add whimsy. Photo above shows detail. Collection of Lesley Litzenberger.

Using historic symbol for hospitality, hand-pieced Pineapple crib quilt is complex variation of popular Log Cabin pattern. Design: Sandi Fox.

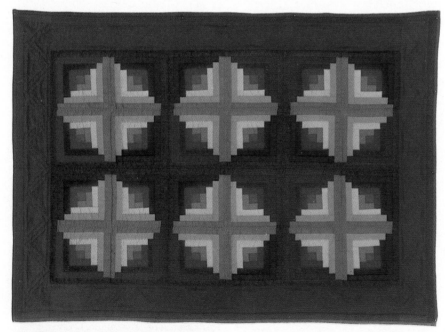

Traditional Amish colors combine in contemporary wall hanging of Light and Dark Log Cabin. Quilting ornaments border. Design: Sara Halpern Robb.

Variations on a theme — contemporary interpretations of classic Log Cabin patterns

Opposite pairs of light and dark logs in individual blocks create Straight Furrow design of this contemporary cradle quilt, pieced and stitched entirely by hand. Design: Sandi Fox.

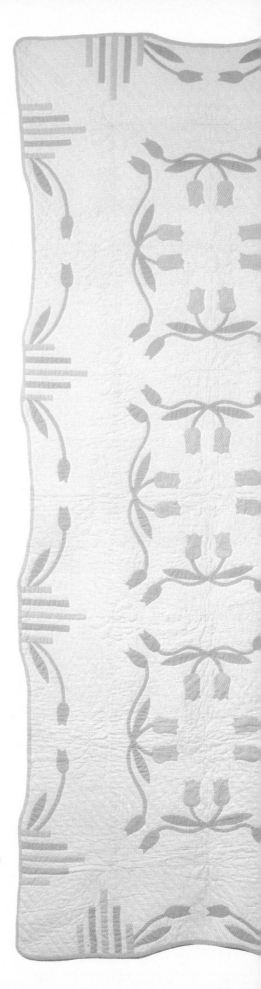

When set together, Spice Pink's blocks and dividers combine to form four floral wreaths. Design: Lena Moses.

Contemporary Plumeria design by Kepola Kakalia exhibits Hawaiian contour quilting, bold pattern, and single vivid color applied to pale background. Collection of Sylvia Moore.

Appliqué quilt designs, abloom with floral motifs and springtime colors

Tulips bloom the year around on this pastel-pretty appliqué quilt, circa 1930. Delicate quilting and striking scalloped borders accentuate its feminine air. Collection of Once Upon A Quilt.

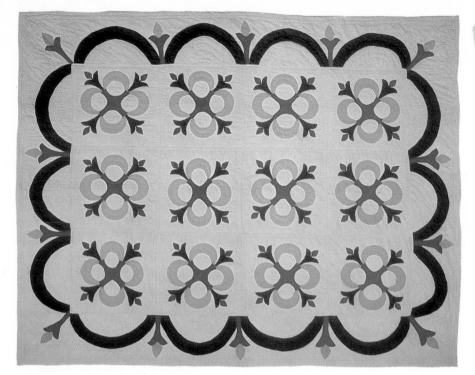

Exuberant, brightly colored pattern marks Pennsylvania Dutch quilt from late 1800s. Collection of Margaret Baer.

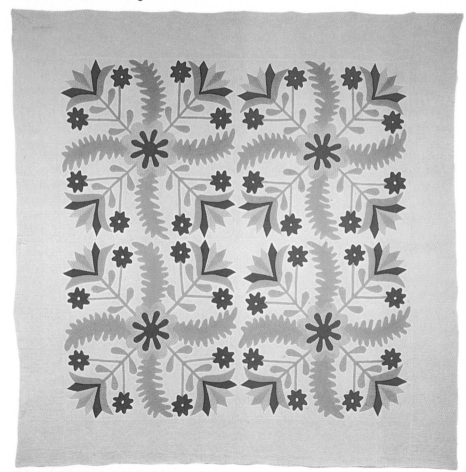

Princess Feather, a popular pattern, is further enlivened with floral motifs in Pennsylvania quilt, circa 1900. Collection of Priscilla Wrubel.

Bright colors, stylized shapes stand out in bold appliqué quilts

Contour quilting outlines appliqué shapes in delightful Pomegranate quilt, circa 1932. Detail shows closely spaced stitching necessary to secure cotton batting. Design: Fern Purdy.

Contemporary and traditional
appliqué designs were used by Santa
Clara Valley Quilt Association members
to create this friendship quilt. Color
coordination and communal quilting
unify stitchery bouquet.

Friendship, album, or community quilts — group efforts that culminate in magnificent, memorable quilts

Sixteen artists designed blocks for Oakland landmark quilt; other League of Women Voters members set quilt and added Wild Goose Chase border. Enlarged detail depicts notable city scenes. Design: Lois Campbell.

Distribution of color values creates a pattern in motion. Design: Grace Earl.

Contemporary quilts reflect diversity and imagination in the state of the art

A pattern to puzzle over, quilt named "Dusk 1981" subtly blends colors, shapes, and sizes in a diagonal progression. Design: Linda MacDonald.

Grandmother's Farm quilt graphically depicts rural setting. Contoured fields radiate from red-roofed house; top of quilt shows steep hillside vineyard. Design: Verena Levine.

Extravagantly stitched, this antique
Amish quilt today acts as wall hanging.
Pattern is Baskets or Cake Stand.
Collection of Mary Mashuta.

Wonderful on walls, quilts effectively display graphic colors and designs

Diagonal bands of warm and cool colors create an artist's palette in this contemporary hanging composed of triangles. Design: Victoria Ann Philp.

Variable Star's blocks glimmer softly against rich black background of Amish quilt, circa 1880–1900. Collection of Ruth Soforenko.

Ocean Waves pattern flows across bed in Pennsylvania quilt, circa 1880. Collection of Mary Strickler's Quilt Gallery.

Hawaiian designs splash across accent pillows. Closely set hand quilting outlines Breadfruit and Bluebell appliqué. Collection of Jini Johnson.

Century-old Double Irish Chain quilt takes on new role in contemporary dining setting. Collection of Dr. Deborah Rose.

Quilting moves from beds to walls to tables — and, compressed, to pillows

Pieced and plain blocks set on point make up intricate Double Nine-Patch, from late 1800s. Delicate feather quilting adds texture to white areas. Collection of Dr. Deborah Rose.

Quilt Gallery **87**

Index

Boldface numbers refer to color photographs; names of quilt designs appear in italics.

Varied colors and intriguing design of Churn Dash crib quilt, set on point, will fascinate several generations of children. Design: Sara Halpern Robb.